THORVALDSEN'S
MUSEUM

COPENHAGEN
1961

TRANSLATION BY INGEBORG NIXON, M.A., PH.D.

GENERAL INFORMATION

Hours of   Summer (May 1st to September 30th) 10 to 4.
Admission: Winter (October 1st to April 30th) 10 to 3.

Admission free on Sunday, Wednesday, and Friday; other days 1 krone.
The Museum is closed on June 5th, and on Christmas Day.

The Office of the Museum is on the first floor (tel. PAlæ 5097).

Plaster casts of Thorvaldsen's sculptures are *on sale* in the basement of the Museum (Note: original size only). An illustrated catalogue giving dimensions and prices is available on application to the custodian, or the Museum office.
Catalogues (Danish, English, French, and German), postcards, slides, and Museum publications are on sale at the entrance.
Conducted tours of the Museum (free) every Sunday at 10.30. Lectures illustrated by slides, art films with accompanying lectures, and occasionally concerts, are given every spring and autumn; these are announced by posters and by notices in the daily papers.

The collections are distributed as follows:

Ground Floor: Marble sculptures and original models by Thorvaldsen.

First Floor: Rooms XXII–XXXII: Thorvaldsen's collections of contemporary paintings (Rooms XXXI–XXXII also contain personal relics);
Rooms XXXIII–XXXIV: Thorvaldsen's sketch models for statues and reliefs;
Rooms XXXV–XL: Thorvaldsen's collections of Egyptian, Greek and Roman antiquities;
The corridors: Thorvaldsen's original models for statues and reliefs.

Basement: Rooms XLIII–XLVI: early works by Thorvaldsen;
The corridors, Rooms XLIX and LX–LXI, and the storage corridor: Thorvaldsen's collections of plaster casts of antique sculpture;
Rooms L–LV: the rest of Thorvaldsen's collection of paintings;
Room LVI: a selection of Thorvaldsen's collection of drawings by contemporary artists;
Rooms LVII–LIX: personal relics of Thorvaldsen, and
Room LIX: his collection of death-masks.

*   *   *

THORVALDSEN'S MUSEUM

is the property of the City of Copenhagen. The inscription on the side of the building facing the palace church gives the following account of its origin:

THORVALDSEN DECIDED IN THE YEAR 1837 IN ROME THAT HIS WORKS, COLLECTIONS AND FORTUNE SHOULD GO TO HIS NATIVE CITY CO-PENHAGEN AND THAT WITH THEM SHOULD BE ESTABLISHED A SEPARATE MUSEUM

BY MEANS OF CONTRIBUTIONS FROM KING FREDERIK VI AND KING CHRISTIAN VIII, FROM THE CITY OF COPENHAGEN AND FROM FELLOW CITIZENS OF EVERY RANK THE TASK WAS COMPLETED 1848

The building was designed by the architect M. G. Bindesbøll, and erected under his direction. The work was begun in 1839. When the building had already taken shape the desire was voiced that in addition to housing Thorvaldsen's works and collections it should also be his final resting-place. When his consent had been given to this, a sunken burial chamber was built under the centre of the courtyard, decorated with white lilies on a blue ground by the landscape painter H. C. From. Thorvaldsen's coffin was placed in it on September 6th 1848. The granite edging of the tomb bears the following inscription:

BERTEL THORVALDSEN
B. 19TH NOVEMBER 1770, D. 24TH MARCH 1844

During Thorvaldsen's lifetime the façades of the building were of undecorated plaster. It was not until two years after his death that Bindesbøll suggested that they should be ornamented with a frieze of figures. The idea was Bindesbøll's; he is believed to have given instructions for the subjects of the figure scenes, and how they were to be placed on the walls. The composition and execution are the work of Jørgen Sonne, under whose direction the frieze was made in 1846-48 and 1850. The technique used is unusual, the murals being constructed of tinted cement plaster applied direct to the walls.

The side facing the canal shows Thorvaldsen's arrival in Copenhagen in 1838. Facing the palace church is the frigate Rota, from which his works are being unloaded. The side facing the palace shows the transport of the works to the Museum.

The decorations on the walls facing the courtyard were carried out during the summer and autumn of 1844. The bay-trees, oaks, and palms are the work of the landscape painter H. C. From, while the frieze with the chariot-driving genii is the work of the German sculptor Johann Scholl (the horses, which were originally made from a drawing by Jørgen Sonne, were altered by Axel Johansen during restoration in 1936-40).

The bronze group above the main entrance – Victory reining in her horses – was presented by Christian VIII. It was modelled by H. V. Bissen, who used a sketch by Thorvaldsen for the figure of the goddess, and one of his models for the second horse from the left (No. 125, p. 33). The reliefs on the corner pilasters were carved in sandstone by Johann Scholl from models by H. E. Freund. They were originally partly painted.

For the ceiling decorations Bindesbøll employed a number of artists and young academy students, of whom G. C.

Hilker, Christen Købke, Jørgen Sonne, G. C. Freund, Heinrich Hansen, A. P. Madsen, and C. F. Sørensen are the best known. Bindesbøll was the moving spirit of the undertaking. His various helpers worked more or less independently under his leadership, and occasionally from his personal designs. His ability to guide and inspire them is legendary. Bindesbøll's decorative skill was also displayed to a special degree in the mosaic patterns of the floors; an often all too little noticed, but in fact very important part of the harmonious whole formed by the interior of the Museum.

On September 17th 1848, the tenth anniversary of Thorvaldsen's return from Italy, the city council officially took over Thorvaldsen's art collections, and on the following day the Museum was opened to the public.

*   *   *

As already mentioned, the Museum contains both Thorvaldsen's own works and his collections. The former consist of a large number of drawings (not exhibited), many sketch models, most of his original full-scale models, a number of casts, marbles made under his direction and finished by him, and marble copies made by various artists after his death.

Thorvaldsen's collections are very extensive, and provide interesting evidence of his wide artistic taste. They include works from ancient Egypt, antique glass, antique and oriental bronzes, Greek and Roman marbles, large collections of gems and coins, especially Greek, a fine collection of ancient vases, and various objects in terracotta. But the outstanding feature is the collection of paintings. Though it includes a few Renaissance paintings, the main emphasis is on the art of Thorvaldsen's own day, of which it gives an excellent impression. There are also important collections of water-colours, drawings, engravings, books, and casts of antique sculptures.

There is some doubt as to the date of Thorvaldsen's birth. He himself and his contemporaries believed that he was born in Grønnegade in Copenhagen on the 19th of November 1770. Later research has produced some evidence that he was born at the Royal Lying-in hospital on November 13th 1768, but the evidence is not conclusive, and as yet we must continue to accept the date regarded as correct in his own day. His father, *Gotskalk Thorvaldsen,* was an Icelandic immigrant of an old family, the son of a clergyman, and a woodcarver by profession. His mother's name was *Karen Dagnes;* she was the daughter of a schoolmaster in Jutland. Thorvaldsen's life was a romance, not unlike that of Hans Andersen. It is a tale of how a little Copenhagen street urchin attained the greatest reputation and position in society a sculptor could achieve at that time, a tale of the indomitable energy to be found in a born genius when it is united with character, and of the way a talent can flower if it appears at the right moment of time.

CHILDHOOD AND YOUTH IN COPENHAGEN

Thorvaldsen's home was poor. His father was an inferior woodcarver, struggling with competitors, and according to tradition fond of a glass. His mother is said to have been "a pretty, plump little person" in her youth. Thorvaldsen looked like her, and she was devoted to him. Later in life she became slovenly, and her house untidy.

These conditions had their effect on the boy. He soon

Thorvaldsen's first name is correctly Bertel (a Danish form of Bartholomew). In Italy his name was (incorrectly) rendered as Alberto. He assumed this as long as he was abroad; hence his signature AT.

showed the tenacity and tough endurance that were to be a feature of his whole life. At the age of twelve he was already helping his father with the woodcarving, and he soon surpassed him in skill. It is questionable whether he ever had any regular schooling, but as early as possible, in 1781, he entered the Academy of Fine Arts, the lowest classes of which were at that time intended for craft apprentices. In time, as Thorvaldsen grew up, increased in skill, and attained the guild privileges that accompanied the gold and silver medals of the Academy, he strengthened his father's position at his place of work, and improved the lot of his family to a large extent.

The Academy was quite aware of Thorvaldsen's abilities. His teacher was the sculptor *Johannes Wiedewelt*. But the great man at the Academy at that time, N. Abildgaard the painter, took him under his wing and made use of his help in the interior decoration of one of the Amalienborg palaces. Thorvaldsen became his pupil rather than the pupil of the professor of sculpture. His art training, which ended with the supreme gold medal in 1793, and his development, took place hesitantly and with a certain doubt. He needed time to grow. Moreover, he had to work for his living, partly by helping his father to carve figureheads for ships and mirror frames for drawing-rooms, partly by drawing or modelling portraits, and drawing vignettes for books. The last happy years before he went abroad, free from financial worry, were won by his own hard work.

Thorvaldsen's first youthful works all belong to the ebbing 18th century style, a rococo art with marked classicistic tendencies. A number of reliefs by him are known, e. g. *The Seasons* and *The Hours* (for Amalienborg, in collaboration with Abildgaard), classical in style, and several portraits, especially the grandiose rococo bust of the statesman

A. P. Bernstorff, which won him the favour of that great man. These years are of importance because they saw the creation of Thorvaldsen's fundamental character. He was a dreamer, but his childhood contained the seeds of that worldly wisdom that later made him an excellent strategist in the complicated matters of life, and he became accustomed to the industry that was characteristic of him to the end. The pressure of external circumstances shaped a spirit that was typically Scandinavian and especially Danish, marked by fluctuating and varying moods, a combination of weakness and strength, without clear-cut contours, but with the stubborn endurance that achieves its aim and knows how to hold on. The keynote of this spirit was gravity. As a young man, Thorvaldsen could not understand that an adult human being could laugh.

ROME 1797-1819

In 1796 Thorvaldsen won the Academy's travelling scholarship. Through the patronage of Bernstorff he was able to travel to Italy on the naval frigate *Thetis,* under the command of Captain *Lorents Fisker.* He embarked on August 29th, and on March 8th 1797 he arrived in Rome. Later he celebrated this day as his "Roman birthday"

His new surroundings made an overwhelming impression upon him. One of his prominent qualities was an exceptional receptiveness, which made up for the gaps in his education. He is described as thirsty for knowledge; he absorbed facts and impressions, and he was fortunate in that intelligent, talented men helped him at decisive moments in his development, and gave him what he needed.

His encounter in Rome with the Holstein-born painter *A. J. Carstens* was of importance for his art, but just as Abildgaard had been his guide in the Academy years, so it was the

Danish antiquarian *Georg Zoëga,* Denmark's diplomatic re-
representative at the Holy See, who gave him a detailed knowledge of ancient classical art and its spirit, and whose criticism probably influenced his point of view. By order of
the Academy he taught himself marble cutting by copying
antique busts. He also made a few other things, including a
sketch model for a group of *Achilles with the dying amazon
Penthesilea,* which is among his most brilliant works. But
he did not produce much. It was a period of growth, of the
formation of an artist.

It often proved to be the case in Thorvaldsen's life that
such periods were unproductive, but that when the time
was ripe his mind would find release with amazing strength
and ease. This happened near the end of his scholarship stay
in Rome, when more or less in despair he modelled the
statue of *Jason* towards the end of the year 1802. It became
a manifesto of his art. With it he perfected the classicist tendencies that had prevailed in Rome since the middle of the
18th century, and approached the Graeco-Roman ideals
more nearly, both in style and in spirit, than any other
sculptor had done. The way had been paved for this work
to a very high degree. The Italian sculptor *Canova,* the great
name of that period, at once recognized its importance, and
with one stroke the basis of Thorvaldsen's fame was
established.

For financial reasons Thorvaldsen now had to decide to
go home. At the last moment the English conoisseur and
collector *Thomas Hope* commissioned the Jason in marble,
the financial situation was saved, and Thorvaldsen was
able to stay in Rome. The Denmark of Frederik VI would
not have been in a position to support the work of a great
sculptor and give him possibilities for developing. Rome, on
the other hand, was the metropolis of the whole world,

where all roads led, and where art lived on the commissions left by great men on their travels, not least by rich Englishmen. Even though Thorvaldsen created his fame by his own genius, it was to a large extent England that financed it. Orders soon poured in, and he stayed in Rome till 1819, tied down by an unceasing production. Unaffected by the great events of the Napoleonic Wars, which afflicted Rome also in the form of war, plague, and unrest, he created an art that expresses the eternal ideals of human perfection within the laws of beauty and harmony.

This period produced most of Thorvaldsen's most characteristic works. The statues include *Cupid and Psyche* (1807), *Adonis* (1808), *Mars and Cupid,* the nude portrait statue of little *Georgiana Russell* (1814-15), the seated figure of Countess *Ostermann* in an Empire gown (1815), *Venus* (1813-16), *Hebe* (1816), *Ganymede with the Eagle* (1817), *A Shepherd Boy* (1817), *The Dancer* (1817), *Mercury killing Argus* (1818), the standing figure of Madame *Barjatinsky,* a characteristic representation of the prevailing feminine ideal (1818), *Hope* (1817), *The Graces and Cupid* (1817-19), and the *Lion Monument in Lucerne* (1819).

This was accompanied by an extensive production of reliefs. For Thorvaldsen's treatment of relief style *Brisëis led away from Achilles* (1803) had a significance corresponding to that of *Jason.* Later followed *A genio lumen* (1808), the *Auguste Böhmer* (c. 1812) and *Bethmann-Hollweg* (1814) monuments, with the fine representation of the genius of Death, *Night* and *Day* (1815), and *Priam and Achilles* (1815), which shows his relief style at its height. His many *Scenes from Cupid's Activities* were begun about 1809, but it was the frieze *Alexander the Great's Triumphal Entry into Babylon* that established his reputation. It was commissioned as decoration for the Quirinal Palace in Rome on the occasion of Napoleon's expected visit in 1812. Although it is nearly 35 metres long, Thorvaldsen modelled it in only three months, and under difficult conditions at that. His contemporaries were astounded at this achievement, and in honour of it christened him "the patriarch of basrelief".

Some of these works were created as Thorvaldsen's contribution to the treatment of art motifs prominent at that time, often inspired by ancient sculptures, by Carstens or other artists, and not least by rivalry with the great Italian *Canova*. Although Thorvaldsen took a highly critical view of Canova, he nevertheless modelled himself upon him in certain ways. They inspired one another. In a number of works they have both treated the same subject and the same motif; Thorvaldsen's work developed outwardly along the same lines as Canova's; and just as Canova founded and erected a museum for his own art in his native town of Possagno, so the idea of Thorvaldsen's Museum originated with Thorvaldsen himself. But Thorvaldsen, who was nearly ten years younger, was more advanced and flexible in his appreciation of the classical prototypes; he was even attracted by early Greek archaic art, which at that time was little known and not highly estimated. In 1816 he restored the recently unearthed gable groups from the Temple of Aphaia on Aegina (now in the Glyptothek in Munich) for King Louis of Bavaria. It was one of his finest artistic achievements, even though the result is archaeologically open to criticism. Archaic art also supplied him with the motif for *Hope,* which is both Greek in spirit, and a romantic symbol.

This period shows an increasing understanding on Thorvaldsen's part of the plastic values attained by classical antiquity. It is predominantly Roman in *Adonis,* Greek in *Hebe, Priam and Achilles,* and *Hope.* But this did not in the least prevent Thorvaldsen from taking motifs from ordinary

life, as he did with *The Shepherd Boy* and *Mercury,* treating
them in a way that does not differ essentially from his other
works. The foundation of the whole was Thorvaldsen's own
Danish spirit and its moods. Unless one realizes this it is impossible to understand the striking harmony of his work,
and the wide range often to be seen in his ability to create
symbols. However objectively he worked with plastic values, aiming at the realization of a classical ideal, there is little
doubt that many of his works originated secretly in inner
personal experiences, which crystallized symbolically, and
found release in the form of art.

German romanticism in Rome probably helped to preserve this lyrical element in Thorvaldsen's mind. The German artists belonged to his circle, some of them were even
on occasion fellow workers, and at one time he cultivated
a type of drawing very closely associated with the German
romantic school, and very different from his other extant
designs and sketches.

PERSONAL CIRCUMSTANCES

Thorvaldsen had a brilliant career, but in his private life he
did not altogether escape unhappiness. The honours that
were showered upon him throughout his life, without however affecting him in the least or making the slightest difference to his unassuming character, began in 1804 with the
title of professor at the Academy in Florence. In 1805 he was
appointed a member of, and professor at, the Academy in
Copenhagen at one and the same time – something quite
exceptional – and the appointment was kept vacant until he
returned to Denmark for good, thirty-three years later. In
1808 he also became a member of, and professor at the
Accademia di San Luca in Rome, an important post carrying a substantial salary. But in his personal life he suffered

grief. His parents died before he was able to see them again, and he never experienced lasting happiness in love. At an early age he fell in love with an Italian woman, *Anna Maria Magnani,* at that time the wife of the German archaeologist Wilhelm Uhden, who was the Prussian Ambassador to the Holy See. After her separation from her husband she and Thorvaldsen lived together, not without stormy passages. Since she was a Catholic they were unable to marry. She bore him a son, probably in 1806, and in 1813 a daughter, *Elisa.* He was deeply affected by his son's death in 1811. In 1818 his intimate acquaintances tried to bring about his engagement to a Scottish lady, *Frances Mackenzie of Seaforth,* but Thorvaldsen broke off the connection in a way that does him little credit. There was nearly a scandal, and Thorvaldsen himself suffered from a secret sense of guilt for many years.

As a result of this and other troubles, Thorvaldsen yielded in 1819 to the steadily growing demands from Denmark that he should come home. His help was wanted with the decoration of C. F. Hansen's new buildings, Christiansborg Palace and its church, the Law Courts, and the Church of Our Lady in Copenhagen. On July 14th 1819 he left Rome. The journey was a triumphal progress. The newspapers treated it as an important event, and on his way through Italy, Germany, and Poland Thorvaldsen received many commissions, and made contracts for the delivery of several impressive monuments. In Copenhagen, where he was extravagantly fêted, he modelled the royal family, and agreed to make the group of *The Preaching of John the Baptist* for the pediment of the Church of Our Lady, and *twelve apostles* for the interior of the church. On December 16th 1820 he arrived in Rome once more.

ROME 1820-38

Thorvaldsen's practice had gradually increased, and when he returned with all these important commissions it developed still more rapidly. One might almost say that his studio became an art factory. Many marble sculptors and young artists were employed there, working from his designs and under his supervision. He himself was always present, correcting, suggesting, or intervening personally when necessary. Even his great statues were produced in several marble replicas; for instance, it is recorded of the bust of the emperor *Alexander I*, which he modelled in Warsaw in 1820, that orders were received "in such numbers that for the first few years after his return to Rome Thorvaldsen employed two of his marble workers on this alone" (Thiele). His studio was at that time one of the sights of Rome, to be visited by all prominent tourists, who often left new commissions. The ability shown by Thorvaldsen in building up this practice without working capital, in managing it, and in guiding his assistants so that they worked in his own spirit, is another remarkable feature of his genius.

The twenties and thirties saw the creation of the great monuments by which Thorvaldsen's name and reputation are known throughout the world. For Poland he made Count *W. Potocki's* monument in Cracow Cathedral (1821), *Copernicus* (1822), and the equestrian statue of Prince *Jozej Poniatowski*, the national monument of the Polish people (1826-27), both in Warsaw; for Germany, the Duke of *Leuchtenberg* (1827), and the equestrian statue of Elector *Maximilian* (1833-35), both in Munich, *Gutenberg* in Mainz, made by H. V. Bissen from Thorvaldsen's design (1833-34), and *Schiller* in Stuttgart, a true statue of a poet, and one of Thorvaldsen's finest achievements (1835); on the other hand, a *Goethe* monument for which he made a design came to nothing. Italy acquired the monument to the painter *Appiani* in the Brera Gallery in Milan, with the large and handsome relief of the three Graces (1821), the statue of *Conradin,* the last of the Hohenstaufens, commissioned by King Ludwig of Bavaria for the church of S. Maria del Carmine in Naples (1836), and *Pope Pius VII's monument* in St Peter's, ordered and paid for by Cardinal Consalvi (1824-31). The last item is a remarkable testimony to Thorvaldsen's reputation, as the only instance of a heretic's being allowed to create a papal monument in the very citadel of Catholicism. England acquired the statue of *Byron* (1831) at Trinity College, Cambridge. But Thorvaldsen's greatest achievement was the adornment of the *Church of Our Lady* in Copenhagen, comprising the statue of Christ (1821), the twelve apostles (1821-27 and 1842), the John the Baptist group (1821-22), the font (the kneeling angel, c. 1828), and the two friezes in relief of the journey to Calvary, and the entry into Jerusalem (both 1839-40).

To these must be added, as commissioned work, an enormous number of reliefs, including the greater part of his Cupid scenes, *The Ages of Love* (1824), the two curious pictures of the *Hylas* legend (1831 and 1833), the four round allegories of *The Ages of Life and the Seasons* (1836), and *Hector's Farewell* (1837). Many visitors were modelled by Thorvaldsen, and there grew up a gallery of busts which is only nowadays appreciated at its true worth.

The most important feature of this period is the religious sculptures. His contemporaries were surprised that Thorvaldsen the Greek should master Christian art also, but his style became the norm within this field almost up to the present time, and the brilliant simplicity of the attitudes places his Christ and his Angel holding a font in the first

rank of his works. His Christ is indeed the only representation of the Saviour that has a power of appeal everywhere
in the world. It represents the heart of religion: the love of
mankind, and of all that lives.

OLD AGE IN DENMARK

After twenty years of intense activity Thorvaldsen at last
yielded to the pleas from Denmark that he should come
home for good. The government sent a man-of-war to
fetch him. On August 8th 1838 at Leghorn he embarked on
the frigate *Rota,* under the command of Captain H. B. Dahlerup, and on September 17th he saw Copenhagen again. His
arrival was a national event of almost legendary character.

In order to gain a little peace in the face of the general
homage, and the social life that accompanied it, he accepted
an invitation from Baroness *Stampe* of Nysø near Præstø, in
the south of Zealand. Apart from one more visit to Italy,
from May 1841 to October 1842, he divided his time between Nysø and his official residence at Charlottenborg,
where in 1843 he modelled the colossal statue of *Hercules*
for Christiansborg. At Nysø he found not only peace in
which to work – in the studio built for him in the beautiful
garden he executed his *Self-Portrait Statue* (1839), and the
two reliefs showing life at Nysø as he knew it (1840) – but
also a home, he who had always had an uncomfortable
bachelor existence; and in his conversations with Baroness
Stampe he was able to take stock of his life. His ardent spirit
obtained peace. He died suddenly, on March 24th 1844, in
his seat at the Royal Theatre, and on September 6th 1848
his coffin was placed in the tomb prepared for him in the
courtyard of the Museum.

HIS ACHIEVEMENT

Taken as a whole, Thorvaldsen's influence on Danish art extended through his pupil H. V. Bissen, and the latter's son Vilhelm Bissen, right up to Kai Nielsen and Utzon-Frank. As a result, Danish sculpture never lost its classical restraint, even during the wildest experiments of naturalism. Obviously, an artist whose reputation has soared to such excessive heights will later suffer fluctuations in estimation. But his sense of rhythm, keen artistic instinct, and ability to translate common human feelings into artistic values have produced works that have a specifically Danish quality about them; and to us here in Denmark his significance at the present day lies perhaps more in the fact that he was Danish than in the fact that he was the finest flower of Roman classicism. In its moderation and artistic tact, his art has kept its attraction for us, and its importance as a restraining and balancing influence.

SIGURD SCHULTZ

THORVALDSEN'S
SCULPTURAL TECHNIQUE

As a boy, Thorvaldsen carved in wood, as did his father. During his years of training at the Academy of Fine Arts he made clay models, which were afterwards cast in plaster. In the case of two larger figures of this period we know that he constructed them in stucco and stone, working from small sketch models, on the actual spot where they were to stand. If he had been free to choose his own material, he would undoubtedly have preferred marble. In his day plaster was considered lifeless, compared with clay and marble, both of which were regarded as living materials. One of Thorvaldsen's friends used the expression "the cold plaster, that stands between the model and the marble, as death stands between life and resurrection". But Denmark was poor in stone suitable for sculpture, and poor in money to pay for the transport of the precious marble all the way from the south.

It was therefore not until his stay in Rome that Thorvaldsen learnt the technique of marble sculpture. Here it had been common practice since the Renaissance that when a sculptor's work was to be executed in stone he made use of both preliminary drawings, and "bozzetti", small, rough sketches in clay or wax, to serve as models during the carving. At the end of the 18th century another method came into use, which made it possible to leave part of the work to the masons; Canova was probably the first to use it. A full-size plaster model was made, which could then with the help of measurements be transferred to the marble block. Thorvaldsen took up the method, and it was this that made his enormous production possible.

Thorvaldsen generally started work with one or more drawings, roughly executed on any paper available, perhaps the back of an invitation or letter. He then modelled a small clay *sketch model,* and with this before him he executed the *model* proper. In order to support the soft clay, he began by erecting on the modelling stand a skeleton of metal rods and wires, the *armature,* which in the case of statues had to branch right out into the fingers, and to which small wooden crosses were fixed at certain points to grip the clay. He then created the model on this framework, first making the general features with his hands, then the details with modelling tools, and lastly using a wet sponge or brush.

A full-size clay model of this kind can be a most attractive work of art, spontaneous and vivid, but it will not last long if it is not kept permanently covered with damp cloths. If the clay is allowed to dry, the figure will begin to crack or crumble. To preserve it in a more permanent form it is cast in plaster. This is done by covering it with layers of plaster, so as to create what is called a "waste mould", which, when dry, can be divided into halves. It is impossible to remove the clay model from this mould in one piece. It has to be taken out bit by bit, and is destroyed in the process. The two halves of the mould are then joined together once more, and plaster is poured in. When it is dry, the new cast can be freed from the mould, which is carefully chipped away, and thus also destroyed.

This first plaster cast is called the *original model,* and is obviously unique. However, alterations could still be made by removing or adding plaster. The model of "Jason" (ground floor corridor) shows clear traces of changes of this kind.

Thorvaldsen could then place the original model side by side with a block of marble, in order to transfer his work to the block by means of a method known in his day as the *academic method,* because it derives from the French Academy in Rome. A number of points marked on the model by a pencilled cross or a small pin were transferred to the block by means of a measuring frame with plumb-lines hanging from it. With the help of these marks one of the many masons employed in Thorvaldsen's studios could rough-hew the block; Thorvaldsen would then complete the work himself, or allow a sculptor, one of his artist-assistants, to finish it under his direction, he himself often giving it the finishing touches.

For the carving, the pointed chisel, the gradine, and other chisels, and sometimes the drill, were used first, then rasps, and finally abrasives such as sandstone, pumice, and emery. While Canova tried to give the marble a gem-like appearance, and to bring out its translucence by polishing, or rubbing in wax, Thorvaldsen took another view of the material. He let the surface of the stone, the skin of the marble (which later generations have often damaged by too much scrupulous cleaning) appear cool and lustreless, almost rough, only changing to a faint gleam on the forward planes.

If we compare works which we know Thorvaldsen himself carved in marble – or at least retouched – with replicas made by his assistants or pupils, we find that the comparison is always in Thorvaldsen's favour. A posthumous marble such as "Alexander sets fire to Persepolis" (Room xv) has a dry, papery texture when compared with the relief "Cupid with Anacreon" (Room iv) made by Thorvaldsen himself, where the form has a vivid life in the coarse-grained Parian marble. Another fine marble made by his own hand is the bust of Ida Brun (Room xvii), where the austere style is softened by a faintly translucent surface.

The technique described above is in principle the method still used. It is demonstrated in the small exhibition "How a sculpture is made" at the entrance to the Christ Hall (opposite Room XII) with the difference that the measuring-frame with the plumb-lines hanging from it has been replaced by a pointing instrument of a somewhat later date. Another feature of this exhibition is the layer of coloured plaster in the waste mould. It indicates to those chipping away the mould that they are now getting near the original model and must work cautiously.

Further replicas of a sculpture can be obtained by making *casts*, either from the original model or from copies in stone or other materials. Thorvaldsen and his contemporaries used the so-called "piece mould", which can be taken apart, and consists of many moulded pieces of plaster, which are assembled in an enclosing casing, also made of plaster.

A piece mould cast differs from the original model in being covered by a net of "burrs", small plaster ridges which appear during the casting where the pieces meet. These burrs can of course be scraped away from the finished cast, but faint traces always remain, and it is easy accidentally to alter the sculptor's original modelling.

Nowadays a gelatine mould is often used; it is pliable, and can be pulled off the cast when the plaster has hardened. But the mould unavoidably becomes a little blurred after repeated castings, both with piece moulds and with gelatine moulds. The original model is therefore closest to the artist's conception. Even though cast in plaster it is an independent, living work of art.

DYVEKE HELSTED

LITERATURE ON THORVALDSEN
AND THE MUSEUM

A great deal has been written about Thorvaldsen and only a small selection of the literature can be mentioned here. Those interested are referred to the bibliography at the end of the article on Thorvaldsen in Weilbach's Dictionary of Artists, 3rd ed., Vol. 3, Copenhagen 1952.

The main source for the historical facts of his life and work is still *Just Mathias Thiele*'s "Thorvaldsens Biographi", I-IV, Copenhagen, 1851-56 (in German, I-III, Leipzig, 1852-56; a shortened edition in English, London, 1865). The last complete monograph, "Thorvaldsen", I-III, Copenhagen, 1924-30, was edited by *T. Oppermann* (director of the Museum 1921-32). In France *Eugène Plon*'s "Thorvaldsen" appeared in 1867 (Paris) (Italian edition, Florence 1874; English edition London, 1874 and Boston, 1874; German edition Vienna, 1875), in Germany *Adolf Rosenberg*'s "Thorvaldsen" was published (Bielefeld and Leipzig) in 1896 (Künstler-Monographien, hrsg. von H. Knackfuss, XVI), and *P. O. Rave*'s "Thorvaldsen" in 1947 (Berlin). *Erik Moltesen* aimed at a wider public in Denmark with his historical account in broad outline, "Thorvaldsens Museum", Copenhagen, 1927, and *Knud V. Rosenstand* wrote an easily read, popular book, "Bertel Thorvaldsen", 2nd ed. Copenhagen, 1932, in which among other things he attempts to convey Thorvaldsen's character with the help of traditional anecdote material.

Contemporary accounts of Thorvaldsen as a man are to be found in *C. F. Wilckens*' "Træk af Thorvaldsens Konstner- og Omgangsliv" ("Incidents from Thorvaldsen's Artistic and Social Life"), Copenhagen, 1874 (German edition 1875), an amusing little book written by Thorvaldsen's valet and the first custodian of the Museum, but not to be swallowed whole (actually written down by the theatrical historian Thomas Overskou); in addition, *A. Wilde,* "Erindringer om Jerichau og Thorvaldsen ombord paa Fregatten Rota 1838" ("Recollections of Jerichau and Thorvaldsen on board the Frigate Rota 1838"), Copenhagen, 1884, and Baroness *Christine Stampe,* "Erindringer om Thorvaldsen" ("Reminiscences of Thorvaldsen"), Copenhagen, 1912, are important sources. The admiration of his contemporaries is illustrated in *Sigurd Schultz'* "Da Thorvaldsen kom hjem" ("When Thorvaldsen came home"), Copenhagen 1938. Valuable light is thrown on Thorvaldsen's character by *Rikard Magnussen*'s "Thorvaldsen's Livsanskuelse" ("Thorvaldsen's Philosophy"), Copenhagen, 1936, and *Louis Bobé*'s "Thorvaldsen i Kærlighedens Aldre" ("Thorvaldsen in the Ages of Love"), Copenhagen, 1938.

For Thorvaldsen's art, *Julius Lange,* "Sergel og Thorvaldsen", Copenhagen, 1886 (German edition Berlin, 1894) is still a classic. *Emil Hannover,* "Thorvaldsens Værker" ("The Works of Thorvaldsen"), Copenhagen, 1907, is a comprehensive collection of pictures with captions. Special fields are treated in *Albert Repholtz,* "Thorvaldsen og Nysø", Copenhagen, 1911, "Thorvaldsens Tegninger" ("Thorvaldsen's Drawings"), Copenhagen, 1920, by the same author, and "Thorvaldsens Portrætbuster" ("Thorvaldsen's Portrait Busts") by *Johannes V. Jensen* and *Aage Marcus,* Copenhagen, 1926. The best analysis of Thorvaldsen's ability to express his experiences symbolically in his sculptures has been given by *Johannes V. Jensen* in his introduction to the above-mentioned work, and in an essay, "Thorvaldsens Fristelser" ("Thorvaldsen's Temptations"), printed in his book "Form og Sjæl", Copenhagen, 1931. *C. Elling*'s "Thorvaldsen", Copenhagen, 1944, gives a modern evaluation of Thorvaldsen from an art historian's point of view. See also "Danmarks Billedhuggerkunst" ("Sculptures of Denmark"), Copenhagen, 1950, the section on Thorvaldsen by *Else Kai Sass*.

The building of the Museum is described in "Thorvaldsens Musæums Historie" ("The History of Thorvaldsen's Museum") by *C.Bruun* and *L.P.Fenger,* Copenhagen, 1892, which is a source-book. The first keeper of the Museum, the numismatist and archaeologist *Ludvig Müller,* to whom great credit is due for arranging the collections, published a careful descriptive catalogue, "Thorvaldsens Museum", sections 1-5, Copenhagen, 1847-50 (French edition, partie 1-5, 1847-51), which was a standard work in its day and still forms the basis of the catalogue. The most detailed popular guide to the Museum is still *M.Galschiøt,* "Thorvaldsens Museum", Copenhagen, 1895, unfortunately long out of print.

In addition to the brief catalogues, Thorvaldsen's Museum has published a catalogue of the collection of cut gems: "Catalogue of the Antique Engraved Gems and Cameos" by *Poul Fossing,* Copenhagen, 1929. Italian art in the collections is treated in *Mario Krohn,* "Italienske Billeder i Danmark", Copenhagen, 1910, and *Harald Olsen,* "Italian Paintings and Sculpture in Denmark", Copenhagen 1961.

The Museum also issues at intervals "Meddelelser fra Thorvaldsens Museum" ("Reports of Thorvaldsen's Museum"), containing articles on Thorvaldsen's sculptures, the Museum building, its restoration, etc. These publications have appeared in 1917, 1918, 1929, 1931, 1935, 1938, 1942, 1944, 1947, 1948, 1952, 1956, 1959, and 1960.

*   *   *

NOTES ON THE USE OF THE CATALOGUE

This catalogue follows the rooms of the Museum, the numbers of these being generally given in the window recesses, in Roman numerals.

The date given for the sculptures is always that of the modelling.

Where nothing else is stated, the sculpture was made in Rome. It is stated in each case whether the work is the original model, a cast, or a marble.

In the case of marbles known or believed to be executed under Thorvaldsen's direction, and possibly finished by him, his name has been added in brackets. In the case of marble replicas made after Thorvaldsen's death, the name of the artist responsible for the execution, where known, has similarly been added in brackets.

As far as possible, an account has been given of the source of the ceiling motif in every room, and of the artists who took part in this decoration, the account being based on statements in C. Bruun's and L. P. Fenger's "Thorvaldsens Musæums Historie", p. 105, 109-10, 114-15, and on transcripts of financial statements.

Dr Vagn Poulsen, Director of the Ny Carlsberg Glyptotek, Copenhagen, Dr P. J. Riis, Professor at Copenhagen University, and Mogens Gjødesen, mag. art., curator at the Glyptotek, have kindly helped in preparing the antique collection sections of this catalogue.

A number of busts by Thorvaldsen have been identified, and their date determined, by Else Kai Sass, formerly curator at the Museum, now Professor at Aarhus University.

Thanks are also due to Dr T.W. I. Hodgkinson of the Victoria and Albert Museum for invaluable advice in the preparation of this translation.

GROUND FLOOR

THORVALDSEN'S SCULPTURES

VESTIBULE

The ceiling reliefs are by G.C.Freund and F.G.Hertzog,
after Thorvaldsen, with the assistance of G.Hoffmann and the architects
Jens J.Eckersberg and T.Sørensen.

STATUES

113   Nicolaus Copernicus. Original model, 1822. Erected in bronze in Warsaw in 1830. Blown up and carried off by the Germans during the War of 1939-45, but restored by the Poles and re-erected in 1950.

114-16   Gutenberg. On the base: The invention of movable type (115), and the printing press (116). Original models. Modelled by H.V.Bissen according to Thorvaldsen's instructions and under his direction, 1833-34. Erected in bronze in Mainz in 1837.

123   Equestrian statue of Prince Jozef Poniatowski. Original model. Commissioned 1817, final contract 1820. Modelled 1826-27. The statue, cast in bronze, was to have been erected in Warsaw in 1832. This was forbidden by Emperor Nicholas I; he presented it to General Paskewitj, who erected it on his estate Gomel in the province of Mogilev in Russia. In 1922 it was restored to Warsaw, where it was erected in the Saxon Square and ceremonially unveiled on May 3rd 1923. On December 16th 1944 it was blown up by the Germans before they abandoned the city. A new

bronze statue, made after the original model in the Museum, was presented to the city of Warsaw by the Danish government and the Corporation of Copenhagen, and unveiled in Lazienki Park, Warsaw, on February 23rd 1952.

128   Equestrian statue of Elector Maximilian I of Bavaria. The horse is the original model, the rider a cast acquired in 1855. Modelled 1833-35. Erected in bronze in Munich in 1839.

135-37   Schiller. On the base: the poet's apotheosis (135), the genius of Poetry (136), and the Goddess of Victory (137). Original models (the actual statue was acquired by the Museum in 1857). Modelled in 1835. Erected in bronze in Stuttgart in 1839.

142-45   Pope Pius VII. On the sides: two female figures, representing Heavenly Wisdom (143), and Divine Power (144). On the base: the Pope's coat of arms, held by two angels (145). Original models, 1824-31. Erected in marble in St Peter's, Rome, 1831.

156   Eugène de Beauharnais, Duke of Leuchtenberg, stepson of Napoleon I, and Viceroy of Italy. Original model, 1827. Erected in marble on the grave of the Duke in St Michael's Church, Munich, 1830.

BUSTS

212   Count Adam Gottlob Detlef Moltke of Nütschau. Original model, winter 1803-04. In marble in the Kunsthalle, Kiel.

219   Baron Herman Schubart, director general of Danish commercial affairs in Italy. 1804. Marble (Thorvaldsen).

220   Baroness Jacoba Elisabeth Schubart. 1804. Marble (Thorvaldsen).

253   The painter Horace Vernet (cf. No. 254, p. 40). Marble (H. V. Bissen).

258   Sir Thomas Maitland, Lord High Commissioner of the Ionian Islands. Erected in bronze on the island of Zakynthos. Relief No. 600 (see below) was placed on the base of the monument, likewise in bronze. Both were removed by the Italians during the War of 1939-45. The relief has since been found. Original model, 1818.

304   Princess Eudoxia Galitzin. Winter 1803-04. Marble (Thorvaldsen).

RELIEFS

317   Hercules receiving the draught of immortality from Hebe. Original model. Together with 318-320 modelled in 1807-10 for Christiansborg Palace.

318   Hygiea feeding the snake of Æsculapius. Original model. See above.

319   Minerva grants a soul to mankind created by Prometheus. Original model. See No. 317.

320   Nemesis recites the deeds of men to Jupiter. Original model. See No. 317.

503   FRIEZE. Alexander the Great's triumphal entry into Babylon. Cast. Modelled in 1812 for the Quirinal Palace on the occasion of Napoleon's expected visit to Rome.

530   The genius of Government. Original model, 1837.

531   The genius of Justice. Like the preceding item, made for the Maximilian memorial in Munich; not used. Original model, 1837.

600   Minerva protects Virtue and reveals Vice. Original model, 1818. Cf. No. 258 (above).

*   *   *

CORRIDOR

The ceiling decoration, a blue star-sprinkled vault divided by bands with the twelve signs of the Zodiac, is by Heinrich Hansen. The signs of the Zodiac are by F.G.Hertzog. Carl Løffler and E.Fich also took part in the work.

STATUES

5   Mercury about to kill Argus. Original model, 1818.

7   Mars and Cupid. Original model, probably 1810. An adaptation of a statue of peace-bringing Mars, modelled in 1808, known from engravings in Ferdinando Mori: Le Statue e li Bassirilievi del Cavaliere Alberto Thorwaldsen, Rome 1811, Pl. 32, and J. M. Thiele's "Bertel Thorvaldsen og hans Værker", I, Copenhagen, 1831, Pl. XXXIII.

9   Vulcan. Original model, 1838.

29 Cupid and the Graces. Original model, 1817-19.

52 Jason with the Golden Fleece. Thorvaldsen's first important sculpture. Original model, 1802-03.

53 Adonis. Original model, 1808.

55-56 Two caryatids. Modelled in 1813 for a monument in Warsaw. Casts of the marble versions, placed in the throne room of Christiansborg Palace in 1828, destroyed in the palace fire of 1884.

59-70 The preaching of John the Baptist. 1821-22. In bronze above the main entrance of the Church of Our Lady. Nos. 63, an old scribe, 64, a youth, 66, a Pharisee, 68, a boy and girl, and 70, a reclining shepherd, are original models.

71 A standing Roman warrior. Original model. Originally intended for the John the Baptist group.

72 A seated Jew. Original model. Originally intended for the John the Baptist Group.

110 Angel holding a font. Original model, 1823. Standing version. In marble in the National Museum, Stockholm.

119 A dying lion above the royal arms of France. Cut in colossal size in the side of a cliff at Lucerne in memory of the Swiss Guards who fell in Paris during the Revolution, on August 10th and September 2nd and 3rd 1792. 1819. Cast. Cut in the rock by Lucas Ahorn of Constance; completed in 1821.

122 A recumbent lion. Original model, 1825.

125 Horse, modelled for the Poniatowski monument. Used by H. V. Bissen for the quadriga of Victory on the roof of the Museum. Partly an original model, 1822-23.

129 Horse, modelled for the monument of Maximilian of Bavaria. Partly an original model, 1832-33.

146 Angel. Original model, 1830. Placed in marble on the monument of Pope Pius VII in St Peter's, Rome.

147 Angel. Original model, 1830. See No. 146.

155 Count Wlodzimierz Potocki. Original model, 1821. In marble on the Count's tomb in the cathedral on Wawel Rock in Cracow. Cf. No. 627 (p. 38).

162 Thorvaldsen leaning on the statue of Hope. Modelled at Nysø in 1839. Cast. Cf. No. 46 in Room VIII.

BUSTS

186 St Apollinaris, bishop, and patron saint of Ravenna. Original model, 1821.

187 The mathematician Leonardo Pisano (1180-1250). Made for "Protomoteca Capitolina", a collection of the busts of famous men, on the Capitol in Rome. Marble (Thorvaldsen).

189 Elector Maximilian I of Bavaria. Original model, 1831.

3*

205 Prince Frederik of Augustenborg. 1819. Marble (Thorvaldsen).

211 Count Conrad Rantzau-Breitenburg, a Danish statesman. Original model, 1805.

221A Jacob Baden, professor at the University of Copenhagen. 1806. Marble (Thorvaldsen). Purchased 1924.

223 Thorvaldsen. Self-portrait, 1810. Cast of the marble version made by Thorvaldsen himself, in the Academy of Fine Arts.

233 King Ludwig I of Bavaria as crown prince. Original model, 1818.

240A The writer Christian August Tiedge. Winter 1805-06. Marble (Thorvaldsen). Purchased 1920.

240B The writer Elisa von der Recke. Winter 1805-06. Marble (Thorvaldsen). Purchased 1920.

247 The Grand Duchess Helen of Russia. Original model, 1829.

252 Napoleon apotheosized as emperor. 1830. Marble (Thorvaldsen). Purchased 1929.

255 Sir Walter Scott. 1832. Cast.

256 Lord Byron. 1817. Marble.

267 Lady Louisa Sandwich. Original model, 1816.

268 "Miss Lucan". Presumably represents a daughter of Richard Bingham, 2nd Earl of Lucan. Original model.

270 Pope Pius VII. Original model, 1824.

271 Cardinal Ercole Consalvi. Original model, 1824.

275 Georg Wilhelm Karl Wilding, Prince of Butera and Radali. 1815. Marble (Thorvaldsen). Purchased 1950.

276 Donna Catharina di Branciforte, Princess of Butera, wife of the above, 1815. Marble (Thorvaldsen). Purchased 1950.

280 Ghazi 'L-Din Haidar, Padishah of Oudh. Original model, 1824.

283 Dr John Wyllie. Original model, 1831. In marble in the town hall of Forfar, Angus, Scotland.

303 Portrait of a man. Original model.

A900 Count Edmund Bourke, Danish Minister in Naples. Cut in marble in 1800 by Thorvaldsen, probably from a model by the Italian sculptor Domenico Cardelli. Presented in 1955 by Madame Wanda Krosinski, Brussels, in memory of her Danish grandmother, Madame Alix Dolez Castonier.

RELIEFS

361 The goddess of Victory. Made for the base of the Potocki monument (cf. No. 155, p. 33), but not used. A partly original model, 1830.

363 The goddess of Victory. Original model, 1830.

420 Venus, Mars, and Cupid in Vulcan's smithy. Mars the original model, the other figures casts. Probably 1814. Adaptation of No. 419, Room IX.

423 Leda and the swan. Original model, Nysø 1841.

487 The sea-goddess Thetis dipping her son Achilles in the Styx. Original model, 1837.

491 Brisëis led away from Achilles by Agamemnon's heralds. Original model, 1837.

500 Hector in Helen's chamber reproaches Paris for his cowardice. Original model, 1837.

504 Alexander in his triumphal chariot greeted by the goddess of Peace. Variation on the central section of the Alexander processional frieze. Used for Count Sommariva's marble version of the frieze at Villa Carlotta by Lake Como (cf. No. 505). Original model.

505 FRIEZE. Alexander the Great's triumphal entry into Babylon. Variation on the frieze in the vestibule (cf. No. 503, p. 31). Cast. Executed in marble in Thor-

valdsen's studio to the order of Count Sommariva for
Villa Carlotta, by Lake Como. The central section
with Alexander, and a few other sections, are however unlike the marble version at Villa Carlotta
(cf. No. 504).

506-7   Sections of the Alexander processional frieze. Used
for the marble version placed in Christiansborg Palace.
506: cast, 507: original model. 1831.

516   Alexander induced by Thaïs to set fire to Persepolis.
Adaptation of No. 515 (p. 65). Original model, 1837.

526   The genius of Poetry. Made for the Schiller monument (cf. No. 135-37, p. 30). Original model, 1835.

529   The genius of Peace and Liberty. Original model,
Copenhagen 1844.

551   Adam and Eve with Cain and Abel. Original model,
1838.

567   The child Jesus in the temple. Original model, Nysø
1841.

568   Christ and the woman of Samaria at the well. Original
model, Nysø 1841.

575-78   The four evangelists, supported by the winged
figures that symbolize them. 1833. Marble.

583   St Luke, with his symbol the ox. Original model.

584   St Luke as the first Christian painter. Original model.

589   Christmas joy in heaven. Nysø 1842. Cast.

603   Hans Madsen, priest of Svanninge, tells Johan Rantzau
of the enemy's plans. Original model, Nysø 1841.
In bronze in Svanninge Church, Funen.

TOMB RELIEFS

593-95   Doomsday angels. Original models, 1842.

611   Raphael crowned with a wreath by the goddess of
Victory, while the genius of Art holds a torch. Made

for Raphael's monument in the Pantheon in Rome, but not used. Original model, 1833.

612 Cardinal Consalvi restores the Papal provinces to Pius VII. Original model. Like the bust No. 271 (p.34), in marble on Consalvi's sarcophagus in the Pantheon; erected 1825.

613 Tobias heals his blind father. Original model, 1828. Made in marble for the tomb of the oculist Vacca Berlinghieri in Campo Santo, Pisa.

616 A brother and sister leave their mother on this earth. Original model, 1835. Made in marble for the monument of Princess Helena Poninska's children in the palace chapel, Czerwonogród (Podolia).

618 Baron Schubart bids farewell to his wife on her deathbed. Original model, 1814. Made in marble for the tomb of Baroness Jacoba Elisabeth Schubart (cf. Room XI, No. 618A).

620 A man clasps the hand of his wife, who stands with covered head before him. Original model, c. 1831-32. Made in marble for the tomb of Sir Charles Drake Garrard of Lamer, in Wheathampstead parish church, Hertfordshire.

621 A mother led away from her son by the genius of Death. Original model, 1816. Made in marble for the tomb of Countess Borkowska in the Dominican church in Lvov.

622 The genius of Death and an elderly kneeling woman on either side of a tombstone. 1818. Cast. Made in marble for the Countess of Newburgh for the tomb of her husband, Anthony Radcliffe, 5th Earl of Newburgh, in the Catholic church of St Richard's, Slindon, Sussex.

623 An elderly woman kneeling between two angels.

Original model, 1828. Made in marble for the tomb of Lady Lawley in Escrick parish church, Yorkshire.

624   A woman ascends to heaven, above the genius of Death. Original model, 1818. Made in marble for the tomb of Baroness Chaudoir.

625   Similar to No. 624. Original model.

627   The genius of Death. Original model, 1829. Made in marble for the tomb of Count Wlodzimierz Potocki in the Wawel cathedral at Cracow. Cf. No. 155 (p. 33).   *   *   *

At the entrance to the Christ Hall is the model arrangement of *the making of a sculpture,* showing the various stages, from the framework, through the clay modelling and casting in plaster (in the so-called waste mould), to the original model. This is made of plaster, and is unique. The stone or metal version is made from it. Below is a complete set of sculptor's tools for working with clay, plaster, and stone.

For further discussion of Thorvaldsen's technique, see the introductory section of this catalogue (p. 21-24).

THE CHRIST HALL

The motif of the arch has been taken from the baths at Pompeii.

STATUES

82 Christ. 1821. Cast after the original model. Erected in marble in the Church of Our Lady, 1839.

86-108 The twelve apostles. 86: Peter. 87: Matthew. 89: John. 91: James the Less. 93: Philip. 96: Thomas. 98: James the Greater. 99: Bartholomew. 101: Simon Zelotes. 103: Paul. 105: Thaddæus. 108: Andrew. Original models, made 1821-27, with the exception of Thaddæus and Andrew, which were modelled in 1842. Marble versions of Nos. 86-103 were placed in the Church of Our Lady in 1839; 105 and 108 were added not later than 1848.

112 Angel holding a font. About 1828. Cast. Erected in marble in the Church of Our Lady in 1839.

RELIEFS

559 FRIEZE. Christ's entry into Jerusalem. Original model, Nysø, 1839-40. Sketch model for the frieze above the main entrance of the Church of Our Lady.

560 FRIEZE. Christ's journey to Calvary. Original model, Nysø, 1839-40. Sketch model for the frieze in the choir of the Church of Our Lady.

564 Christ assigns the leadership of the Church to St Peter. 1818. In marble on the font of the altar of the chapel at Villa Poggio Imperiale, Florence. Cast of the marble version.

569 The Annunciation. Original model, 1842.

570 The Adoration of the shepherds. Original model, 1842.

572 The child Jesus in the temple. Original model, 1842.

573 Christ baptized by John the Baptist. Original model, 1842.

596 The child's guardian angel. Original model, Copenhagen, 1838. Made in marble for the school collecting-box in the Church of Our Lady.

597 Christian charity. 1810. Marble. Made in marble for the almsbox in the Church of Our Lady.

ROOM I

The ceiling decoration was designed and executed by A. F. Behrends, in collaboration with M. M. Goldschmidt, E. Fich, J. J. G. Guntzelnick, and J. P. Rasmussen. The motif has been taken from a Pompeian glass amphora and from a floor mosaic in Goethe's house in Pompeii.

40 STATUE. Ganymede offering the cup. 1804. Marble (Thorvaldsen). Purchased in London 1920.

42 —Ganymede filling the cup. 1816. Marble. An original marble version is in the Hermitage, Leningrad.

224 BUST. The painter C. W. Eckersberg. 1816. Marble (Thorvaldsen). Presented by Eckersberg's daughters 1883.

254 —The painter Horace Vernet. Original model, 1832. The original marble version is in the Musée Calvet, Avignon.

284 —Portrait of a man. Original model.

285 —Portrait of a man. Original model.

327 RELIEF. The genius of Light with Pegasus. Original model. About 1836.

517 —Art and the light-bringing genius. Original model. Presumably a preliminary version of No. 518 (p. 65).

548 —The genius of the New Year. Nysø 1840. Cast.

ROOM II

The ceiling decoration was designed by C. Købke, based on a motif in Diomedes' villa in Pompeii, and executed by Købke in collaboration with J. F. Busch and E. Fich.

27   GROUP. Cupid and Psyche reunited in heaven. 1807. Marble (H. V. Bissen).

426   RELIEF. The Ages of Love. 1824. Marble.

428   —Cupid leaves the bed of the sleeping Psyche. Original model, Nysø 1841.

429   —Psyche with the lamp approaches the sleeping Cupid. Original model, Nysø 1841.

430   —Cupid revives the swooning Psyche. Montenero 1810. Marble (Thorvaldsen). Purchased in London 1926.

585   —Angels singing. 1833. Marble.

587   —Angels playing. 1833. Marble.

ROOM III

The ceiling decoration is by L. Lehmann, Joel Ballin, J. J. G. Guntzelnick, and J. F. Busch. Lehmann painted Aurora leading the horses of the sun, four hovering figures, the quarters of the globe, and the triumph of Galatea in the lunette. The stucco frieze is by Ballin, based on a motif on an ancient bronze bucket.

29A   GROUP. Cupid and the Graces. 1817-19. Marble (Thorvaldsen). Purchased 1952.

245   BUST. Karoline von Rehfues. Original model, 1827.

305   —Portrait of a lady. Original model.

340   RELIEF. The dance of the Muses on Helicon. Modelled at Baron Schubart's villa at Montenero, Leghorn (1804). Altered 1816. Marble (H. V. Bissen).

371   —Cupid feeding Hygiea's snake. 1837. Marble.

375 RELIEF. The Graces with Cupid in chains of roses.
     1831. Marble.

393 —Cupid asks Jupiter that the rose may be the queen
     of flowers. 1831. Marble.

396 —Cupid caressing the faithful dog. 1831. Marble.

397 —Cupid making a net to catch a butterfly, symbol of
     the soul or the fickle heart. 1831. Marble.

ROOM IV

*The four medallions in the ceiling decoration were executed by C. Købke,
from Thorvaldsen's compositions on the story of Cupid and Psyche. The
remaining figures are by F. G. Hertzog. The ornaments were designed and
executed by N. Borggreen, William Hammer, and P. A. Fischer. The
frieze is a copy of a terracotta at Pompeii.*

11   STATUE. Venus with the apple awarded by Paris.
     1813-16. Marble (Thorvaldsen). Purchased in Lon-
     don 1920.

348 RELIEF. Venus rising from the foam. Original model,
     1809.

388 —Cupid the lion-tamer. Original model, 1809.

409A —Cupid and Bacchus. 1810. Marble (T. Stein).

410 —Cupid with a swan, and boys picking fruit – Sum-
     mer. 1811. Marble.

412 —Cupid and the youthful Bacchus treading grapes –
     Autumn. Taken from Anacreontea, Song 17. 1811.
     Marble.

414 —Cupid received by Anacreon – Winter. From Ana-
     creontea, Song 3. 1823. Marble (Thorvaldsen). The
     same poem inspired Hans Andersen to write the
     story of "The Mischievous Boy". Presented by
     Thorvaldsen to Thomas Hope 1828. Purchased in
     England 1917.

ROOM V

*The ceiling decoration and the garlands are by William Hammer. Christen
Købke modelled the central panel, showing Apollo's victory over Marsyas,
the seven smaller panels, and the sacrificing genii, the masks, etc.*

51 STATUE. Jason with the golden fleece. 1802–03. Marble.
Commissioned in 1803 by Thomas Hope, and completed in marble by Thorvaldsen in Rome in
1828. Purchased at the Hope auction in England in
1917, and placed in the Museum in 1920.

249 BUST. Prince Jozef Poniatowski. Original model,
1819.

286 —Portrait of a man. Original model.

489 RELIEF. Brisëis led away from Achilles by Agamemnon's heralds. 1803. Marble (H. V. Bissen).

492A —Priam pleads with Achilles for the body of Hector. 1815. Marble (C. Peters).

493 —Achilles binds the wounds of Patroclus. 1837.
Marble.

495 —Achilles with the dying amazon Penthesilea. 1837.
Marble.

ROOM VI

*The central panel of the ceiling decoration was painted by Christen Købke
after a motif from Nero's Aurea Domus (formerly known as the Baths of
Titus). The ornamentation is by A. P. Madsen.*

38 STATUE. Hebe. 1816. Marble (Thorvaldsen). Purchased in London 1938.

265A BUST. Henry Hope, eldest son of Thomas Hope.
Probably modelled 1821. Marble (Thorvaldsen).
Purchased at the Hope auction in England in 1917.

266A —Younger son of Thomas Hope. Probably modelled

in the winter of 1816-17. Marble (Thorvaldsen).
Purchased at the Hope auction in England in 1917.

321 RELIEF. Hercules and Hebe. Marble.

322 —Æsculapius and Hygiea. Marble.

323 —Minerva and Prometheus. Marble.

324 —Nemesis and Jupiter. Marble.
321-324 were modelled 1807-10 for Christiansborg
Palace.

ROOM VII

*The reliefs of the ceiling decoration were modelled by G. C. Freund,
while the ornaments on the dark background were made by A. P. Madsen.*

6 GROUP. Mars and Cupid, from Anacreontea, Song 45.
Probably 1810. An adaptation of a statue of Mars
the peace-bringer, modelled in 1808, and known
from J. M. Thiele: Bertel Thorvaldsen og hans Værker, 1, Copenhagen 1831, Plate XXXIII. Marble
(H. V. Bissen).

273 BUST. Count G. B. Sommariva, the Italian politician
and art collector. Original model, c. 1817-18.

287 —Portrait of a man. Original model.

486 RELIEF. Perseus on Pegasus rescuing Andromeda.
Nysø 1839. Cast.

499 A —Hector with Paris and Helen. 1809. Marble (H. V.
Bissen).

501 A —Hector's farewell to Andromache. 1837. Marble
(H. V. and Vilhelm Bissen). Presented by Captain
J. C. Jacobsen, of the Carlsberg Breweries.

502 —Homer singing for the people. Original model.
Winter 1836-37.

ROOM VIII

The bacchic scenes in the ceiling decoration are by G.C.Freund,
the ornaments on the dark background by W.Hammer.

46 STATUE. The goddess of Hope holding a bud. 1817.
Marble (H.V.Bissen).

366 RELIEF. The Fates with the thread of life. Original
model, 1833.

367 —Night with her children, Sleep and Death. 1815.
Marble (Thorvaldsen).

368 —Day: Aurora with the genius of Light. 1815. Marble
(Thorvaldsen).
367-368 were presented to the Museum in 1959 by
Henrik Kaufmann, Danish Ambassador to the
United States, in memory of his mother, Mathilde,
née von Bernus (1866-1922), the reliefs having been
in her childhood home, "Schlösschen", Bocken-
heim, near Frankfurt-on-Main, for more than a
century.

402 RELIEF. Cupid collecting shells for a necklace. Original model, 1831.

403 —Cupid charms flowers from stony ground. Original
model, 1831.

ROOM IX

The figures in the ceiling decoration are by G.C.Freund,
the ornaments by C.F.Sørensen and C.Weber.

8 STATUE. Vulcan. 1838. Marble (H.V.Bissen).

237 BUST. Wilhelm von Humboldt, the German statesman and philologist. Original model, 1808.

288 —Count Jurij Alexandrovitch Golovkin. Original
model, 1819.

374 RELIEF. The Graces dancing. Original model.
418 —Cupid stung by a bee complains to Venus. From
       Anacreontea, Song 40. Original model, adapted
       from No. 417, Room XIV.
419 —Cupid's arrows forged in Vulcan's smithy. From
       Anacreontea, Song 45. Original model, probably
       1810.
457 —Hymen. Nysø 1843. Cast.
497 —Ulysses receives the arms of Achilles, awarded to
       him by Minerva, while Ajax departs in despair.
       Centre: the sea-goddess Thetis seated on the grave
       of her son Achilles. 1831. Marble.

ROOM X

*The motif of the ceiling decoration has been taken from the house of the
Labyrinth in Pompeii. The composition is by Carl Løffler, who painted
the six herms. The rest of the ceiling is by C.F. Sørensen and others.*

  4 STATUE. Mercury about to kill Argus. 1818. Marble
       (Thorvaldsen). Purchased in London, 1938.
325 RELIEF. Minerva. Original model. About 1836.
326 —Apollo. Original model. About 1836.
352 —Pan teaching a child satyr to play on a reed pipe.
       1831. Marble.
354 —A bacchante and a child satyr. 1833. Marble.
407 —Cupid and Bacchus. Marble. An adaptation of
       No. 409A, Room IV.
416 —Cupid and Anacreon. Marble. An adaptation of
       No. 414, Room IV.

ROOM XI

The ceiling decoration was designed by W. Henck the architect, and executed by G. C. Hilker and William Klein (ornaments). The motif is from Hadrian's villa.

166 STATUE. Countess Ostermann. 1815. Marble (H. V. Bissen). The original marble version is in the Hermitage, Leningrad.

171 —Princess Barjatinsky. 1818. Marble (Thorvaldsen).

239 BUST. Countess Giovanna Nugent. Original model, probably 1818.

278 —Marchesa Marianna Florenzi. Original model, 1828.

306 —Portrait of a lady. Original model.

A 893 —Thomson Henry Bonar. 1817. Marble (Thorvaldsen). Purchased 1950.

451 RELIEF. Cupid and Hymen. Nysø 1840. Marble (H. V. Bissen).

553 —Rebecca and Eliezer at the well. Original model, Nysø 1840-41.

618 A —Monument of Baroness Jacoba Elisabeth Schubart. 1814. Marble (Thorvaldsen).

ROOM XII

The motif of the ceiling decoration is from the tepidarium of the ancient baths at Pompeii. The figures are by G. C. Freund, the stucco friezes and ornaments by C. Weber, William Klein, and C. F. Sørensen. The principal picture in the centre, the lunettes, etc. are by G. C. Hilker.

124 EQUESTRIAN STATUE. Prince Jozef Poniatowski. Preliminary version of the colossal statue in the vestibule. In part an original model, 1826.

203 BUST. Christian, Duke of Augustenborg. 1819. Marble (Thorvaldsen).

207   BUST. Count A. P. Bernstorff, Danish statesman. Marble (Thorvaldsen, 1804).

221   —F. Siegfried Vogt, titular Councillor of State, chargé d'affaires at Naples. 1837. Marble (Thorvaldsen).

229   —The landscape painter J. C. Dahl. Original model, 1821.

234   —Prince Clemens Metternich. 1819. Marble (Thorvaldsen).

236   —General Prince Karl Philipp von Schwarzenberg, Duke of Krumau. Original model, 1821.

241   —The medallist Henri François Brandt. Original model, probably 1817.

242   —C. H. Donner, merchant and Konferensraad. Original model, Copenhagen 1840.

246   —The Emperor Alexander I. Modelled in Warsaw 1820. Marble (Thorvaldsen). Purchased 1946.

257   —Lord Byron. Original model, 1817.

263   —Edward Divett, of Bystock, Devon. Original model, 1817.

272   —Count G. B. Sommariva. C. 1817–18. Marble.

289   —Sir George Hilaro Barlow, Governor-General of India. 1828. Marble (Thorvaldsen). Presented in 1950 by Victoria, Lady Barlow, England.

290   —Portrait of a man. Original model.

316   RELIEF. Jupiter enthroned between Minerva and Nemesis; below, a sea-god and an earth-goddess. Model for the relief in the pediment of C. F. Hansen's Christiansborg Palace, destroyed by fire 1884.

422   —Cupid on a swan. Original model, Nysø 1840.

614   —Monument of Auguste Böhmer. The departed tends her sick mother. On the sides: Nemesis and the genius of Death. Original models, c. 1812.

615   —Monument of Philip Bethmann-Hollweg, who died

in Florence just before the arrival of his brother, who was hastening to bring him the Emperor of Austria's reward for an act of gallantry. This is represented symbolically in the central relief. The left-hand relief shows Philip's sorrowing mother and sister; on the right Nemesis records his deed, while Florence, where he died, is symbolized by the god of the river Arno. In marble in the family vault of the von Bethmanns and Bethmann-Hollwegs in the churchyard of Frankfurt-on-Main. Original model, 1814.

619 —Monument of the Countess Anna Maria Porro Serbelloni. Her sorrowing husband and children. In marble in the Galleria d'Arte Moderna in Milan. Original model, 1817.

ROOM XIII

The central panel of the ceiling, a scene from a classical play, is by Magnus Petersen from a copy by Christen Købke. The ornaments, the motifs of which are taken from Roman mosaics, were executed by Magnus Petersen together with J. P. Rasmussen and J. J. G. Guntzelnick.

121 STATUE. A recumbent lion. 1825. Marble (Thorvaldsen).

130 —Lord Byron. Original model, 1831. Executed in marble after the modified model No. 132 (p. 59), and placed in Trinity College, Cambridge.

210 BUST. Henrik Hielmstierne, titular Privy Councillor Original model, probably 1812.

260 —Admiral Edward Pellew, later Viscount Exmouth. Original model, 1814.

278A —Marchesa Marianna Florenzi. 1828. Marble (H. V. Bissen).

131 RELIEF. The genius of Poetry. In marble on Byron's monument in Trinity College, Cambridge. 1831. Marble.

343 —Cupid listening to the song of Erato. 1830. Marble.

357-58 —A satyr dancing with a bacchante. Original models, probably Nysø 1840 and 1841.

365 —The Fates with the thread of life. 1833. Marble (H. V. Bissen).

614A —Monument of Auguste Böhmer. C. 1812. Marble (Thorvaldsen).

ROOM XIV

The ceiling decoration is by A. F. Behrends, T. Wegener, and W. Hammer. The motif is from the burial chamber in the pyramid of Cestius.

44 STATUE. Ganymede with Jupiter's eagle. 1817. Marble (Thorvaldsen).

347A RELIEF. Mercury brings the infant Bacchus to Ino. 1809. Marble (T. Stein).

351 —Hebe gives Ganymede the cup and pitcher. Original model, 1833.

389 —Cupid riding on a lion. 1831. Marble.

391 —Cupid writes the laws of Jupiter. 1831. Marble (Thorvaldsen).

417 —Cupid stung by a bee complains to Venus. From Anacreontea, Song 40. 1809. Marble (Thorvaldsen).

424 —A shepherdess with a nest of cupids. 1831. Marble (Thorvaldsen).

484 —Hylas stolen by the water-nymphs. 1833. Marble (Thorvaldsen).

ROOM XV

The ceiling decoration was designed by W. Hammer, and largely executed by him with the help of T. Wegener, Herman Hjernøe, and A. F. Behrends. The motif is from Nero's Aurea Domus (formerly known as the Baths of Titus).

155A STATUE. Count Wlodzimierz Potocki. 1821. Marble (C. Peters). The original marble version was made for the count's tomb in the cathedral on the Wawel Rock, Cracow.

248 BUST. Princess Maria Aleksejevna Narysjkin. Original model.

291 —Count Arthur Potocki. 1829. Original model.

359 RELIEF. Victory recording deeds on a shield. About 1830. Marble.

362 —Victory standing with a shield and palm. Original model. About 1830. Like No. 359 originally intended for the base of the Potocki statue (cf. No. 155A).

364 —Nemesis in a chariot, attended by the genii of Punishment and Reward. Original model, 1834. In marble in the chapel of Julius Mylius, Villa Vigoni, by Lake Como.

514 —Alexander induced by Thaïs to set fire to Persepolis. 1832. Marble (H. V. Bissen).

ROOM XVI

The genii in the ceiling rosettes and the dance of the Muses on Helicon in the lunette of the rear wall were executed by J. F. Busch and N. Borggreen from compositions by Thorvaldsen. The rest of the decoration was executed by W. Hammer and Herman Hjernøe.

22A STATUE. Cupid triumphant, examining the point of his arrow. 1814. Marble (T. Stein).

377-80 RELIEFS. Cupid's dominion over the world. 377: Cupid in heaven, on Jupiter's eagle, with the thunderbolt. 378: Cupid on earth, as the lion-tamer, with Hercules' club. 379: Cupid at sea, on a dolphin's back, with Neptune's trident. 380: Cupid in the underworld, as the tamer of Cerberus, with a pitchfork. This series is also known as The Four Elements. Modelled 1828. Marble.

395 RELIEF. Cupid and Ganymede playing at dice. Motif from a poem by Simonides. 1831. Marble (Thorvaldsen).

454 —Cupid and Hymen spinning the thread of life. 1831. Marble.

ROOM XVII

The ceiling decoration is by C. Weber, G.C. Freund, Joel Ballin, David Jacobsen, and Ludvig Lehmann, the motif from the villa of Diomedes in Pompeii.

53A STATUE. Adonis. 1818. Marble (C. Peters).

218A BUST. Ida Brun. 1810. Marble (Thorvaldsen). Bequest from F. Brun, Chamberlain at the Danish Court, 1902.

235 —Prince Clemens Metternich. Original model, 1819.

245A —Karoline von Rehfues. 1827. Marble (Thorvaldsen). Purchased 1923.

259 —Lord George Granville Leveson Gower, later Duke of Sutherland. Original model, 1817.

480 RELIEF. The centaur Nessus embracing the struggling Deianira. 1814. Marble (Thorvaldsen).

488A —The centaur Chiron teaching Achilles to throw a spear. 1837. Marble (T. Stein).

646A —A mounted hunter. 1834. Marble (C. Peters).

647A —A mounted huntress. 1834. Marble (C. Peters).

ROOM XVIII

The central panel of the ceiling, the Times of Day, is by T.Wegener, the moss wreaths by W.Hammer, the ornaments by N.Borggreen and J.F.Busch.

31 GROUP. The Graces with Cupid's arrow, and Cupid playing on a lyre. 1842. An adaptation of the group in Room III. Marble (H.V.Bissen).

191A BUST. King Frederik VI. Copenhagen 1819. Marble (Thorvaldsen). Purchased 1923.

192A —Queen Marie Sophie Frederikke. Copenhagen 1819. Marble (Thorvaldsen). Purchased 1923.

193A —Princess Caroline, daughter of Frederik VI. Copenhagen 1819. Marble (Thorvaldsen). Purchased 1922.

195 —Princess Vilhelmine Marie, daughter of Frederik VI. Probably 1828. Marble (Thorvaldsen).

279 —Vittoria Caldoni from Albano. 1821. Marble (Thorvaldsen). Purchased 1947.

307 —Jane Craufurd. 1818. Marble (Thorvaldsen). Presented 1953 by Brigadier-General Sir Standish G.Craufurd, Bart. Damaged by fire.

328-36 RELIEFS. The Muses. 328: Clio. 329: Euterpe. 330: Thalia. 331: Melpomene. 332: Terpsichore. 333: Erato. 334: Polyhymnia. 335: Urania. 336: Calliope. Original models, about 1836.

337 RELIEF. Mnemosyne, mother of the Muses, with Harpocrates. Original model, about 1836.

525 —The genii of the three fine arts (Painting, Architecture, and Sculpture). Original model, Nysø 1843.

ROOM XIX

*The ceiling decoration is by David Jacobsen, Ludvig Lehmann and
P. A. Fischer.*

176A STATUE. A shepherd boy. 1817. Marble (Thorvaldsen). There is a marble version in the Hermitage,
Leningrad. Purchased 1952.

406   RELIEF. Cupid holding out a rose and concealing
thistles. Original model, 1837.

421   —Cupid riding on a swan. Original model, Nysø
1840.

482   —Hylas stolen by the water-nymphs. 1831. Marble.

638-41   RELIEFS. The Ages of Man and the Seasons. 638:
Childhood, spring. 639: Youth, summer. 640:
Manhood, autumn. 641: Old age, winter. Modelled
1836. Marble.

ROOM XX

*The ceiling decoration is by C. F. Sørensen, C. Weber, G. C. Freund,
W. Klein, and Joel Ballin, who also executed the wall-painting.*

162A STATUE. Thorvaldsen leaning on the statue of Hope.
Modelled at Nysø 1839. Marble (H. V. Bissen).

197   BUST. King Christian VIII as heir apparent. Original
model. 1821. Acquired by the Museum 1854.

198   —Queen Caroline Amalie as princess. 1820. Cast.
Acquired by the Museum 1854.

199   —King Frederik VII as a young prince. Original model, Copenhagen 1820.

200   —King Frederik VII, when older. 1828. Marble.

232   —King Ludwig I of Bavaria as crown prince. 1818.
Marble (Thorvaldsen).

281 BUST. The painter Vincenzo Camuccini. 1810. Marble (Thorvaldsen).

342 RELIEF. The Muses of Tragedy and Comedy. Original model, Nysø 1843.

518A —Art and the light-bringing genius. "A genio lumen". 1808. Marble (Thorvaldsen). Presented by Thorvaldsen to Thomas Hope 1828. Purchased in England 1917.

528 —The genii of Poetry and Harmony. Original model, Nysø 1843.

601 —The Graces listening to Cupid's song. 1821. Marble. In marble on the monument of the painter Appiani, in the Brera collection, Milan.

ROOM XXI

The ceiling decoration has been composed after a motif in Nero's Aurea Domus (formerly known as the Baths of Titus.) Jørgen Sonne painted the Madonna and Child, 8 angels, 7 panels with animals, 4 panels with biblical compositions, and the four evangelists. The Flight into Egypt, the Slaughter of the Innocents, and 4 hovering angels, are by T. Wegener. The white angels and the ornaments on a blue background are by A.F.Behrends, W.Hammer, and E.Fich.

150 STATUE. Conradin, the last of the Hohenstaufens. Original model, 1836. Erected in marble on his grave in the church of S. Maria del Carmine, Naples.

152 —King Christian IV. Original model, Copenhagen 1840. The original bronze version (cast and chased by J.B.Dalhoff) is in Christian IV's chapel in Roskilde Cathedral.

164 —Queen Caroline Amalie as princess. Original model, 1827.

191 BUST. King Frederik VI. Copenhagen 1819. Cast.

192 —Queen Marie Sophie Frederikke. Original model, Copenhagen 1819.

193 —Princess Caroline, daughter of Frederik VI. Original model, Copenhagen 1819.

196 —Princess Vilhelmine Marie, daughter of Frederik VI. Original model, probably 1828.

201 —Prince Frederik Vilhelm of Hessen-Philippsthal-Barchfeld, officer in the Danish Army. 1822. Cast.

202 —Princess Juliane Sophie, wife of the above, daughter of Prince Frederik. 1822. Cast.

557 RELIEF. The baptism of Christ. Copenhagen 1820. Cast. In marble in the Church of Our Lady.

558 —The institution of the Sacrament. Copenhagen 1820. Cast. In marble in the Church of Our Lady.

563 —Christ with the two disciples at Emmaus. Nysø 1839. Modelled as an altar-piece for Stavreby (Jungshoved) Church, near Præstø. Cast. Purchased 1845.

599 —Christian Charity united with Faith and Hope. Original model, 1836.

*   *   *

FIRST FLOOR

WORKS BY THORVALDSEN TOGETHER WITH HIS COL-
LECTIONS OF PAINTINGS, DRAWINGS, ANTIQUES,
BOOKS, ETC.

STAIRS

*The ceiling decoration of the vestibule was drawn and painted by J.C.Lar-
sen. The figures in the stairway decoration are by Joel Ballin, the ornaments by H.C.Nickelsen. The motif is from the house of the Labyrinth,
Pompeii; cf. Room X.*

14 STATUE. Hercules. Copenhagen 1843. Original model. In bronze in Prince Jørgen's Courtyard, Christiansborg Palace.

308 BUST. Portrait of a lady. Original model.

312A —The Duchess Wilhelmine of Sagan. 1818. Cast, the
curls on the forehead and temples being added afterwards (cf. No. 312, p. 61). Presented 1909 by Baron
August Binzer, Munich.

398 RELIEF. Cupid caressing the faithful dog. Original
model, 1831.

399 —Cupid making a net to catch a butterfly, the symbol
of the soul or the fickle heart. Original model,
1831.

450 —Cupid and Psyche. Original model, Nysø 1840.

452 —Cupid and Hymen. Original model, Nysø 1840.

456 —Cupid's swan-song. Original model, Nysø 1843.

481 —The centaur Nessus embracing the struggling
Deianira. Original model, 1814.

488 —The centaur Chiron teaching Achilles to throw a
spear. Original model, 1837.

520 RELIEF. The genius of Painting. Original model,
     Nysø 1843.

521 —The genius of Architecture. Original model, Nysø
     1843.

522-23 —The genius of Sculpture. Original models, Nysø
     1843.

527 —The genius of Poetry. Original model, Copenhagen
     1844.

646 —A mounted hunter. Original model, 1834.

647 —A mounted huntress. Original model, 1834.

*   *   *

The *synchronological pillar* is to be found on this floor. It
gives a full survey of Thorvaldsen's life, work, and times
in facts and pictures.

The pillar is divided into narrow vertical panels, each representing one year. When the pillar is turned, Thorvaldsen's period and the events that took place during his lifetime appear collectively in chronological order.

The long *bands* at the top show the lives of Thorvaldsen
and his family, and the periods spent by him in Denmark
and in Italy. Then follow *yellow* slips with details of Thorvaldsen's life, *photographs* of his sculptures, *green* slips showing cultural events, *blue* slips showing political events, and
at the bottom, on *grey* slips, the births and deaths of famous
personages. The *blue band* at the foot of the pillar shows the
reigns of the contemporary Danish kings.

The synchronological pillar was designed by the artist
Poul Sæbye, and completed in 1941.

CORRIDOR

The motif of the ceiling decoration is from Nero's Aurea Domus (formerly known as the Baths of Titus). The work was carried out by Heinrich Hansen, C.F.Sørensen, A.P.Madsen, W.Hammer, William Klein, N.Borggreen, C. Weber, Christian Løffler, E.Fich, M.M.Goldschmidt, and J.J.G.Guntzelnick. J.F.Busch, J.P.Rasmussen, F.C.Lund, P.A.Fischer, and A.F.Behrends are also believed to have taken part.

STATUES.

2 Bacchus. Original model, 1804.

3 Apollo. Original model, 1805.

12 Venus with the apple. Original model, 1813-16.

22 Cupid triumphant. 1814. Cast.

24 Cupid triumphant. 1823. Cast.

26 Psyche with the jar of beauty. Original model, 1806.

28 Cupid and Psyche reunited in heaven. Cupid a cast, Psyche the original model, 1807.

32 Cupid and the Graces. 1842. Cast. Adaptation of No. 29A, Room III.

34 Cupid playing on a lyre. Original model, 1819. Presented by Thorvaldsen to the medallist C. Voigt. Purchased 1882.

36 Cupid standing with his bow. Cast.

37 Hebe. Original model, 1806.

39A Hebe. 1816. Adaptation of No. 37. Possibly the original model. Purchased 1934.

41 Ganymede offering the cup. 1804. Cast.

43 Ganymede filling the cup. 1816. Cast.

45 Ganymede with Jupiter's eagle. 1817. Cast.

47 The goddess of Hope. Original model, 1817.

132 Lord Byron. 1831. Cast, head from the bust No. 257, Room XII, the rest from the original model No. 130, Room XIII. In marble in the library of Trinity College, Cambridge.

167   Countess Ostermann. Original model, 1815.

172   Princess Barjatinsky. Original model, 1818.

173   Georgiana Elizabeth Russell. 1814–15. Cast.

174   A little girl (Jeanina Stampe) represented as Psyche. Original model, Nysø 1840.

177   A shepherd boy. Original model, 1817.

178   A dancer. Original model, 1817.

179   A dancer. Cast. Adaptation of No. 178. Made in marble for Prince Carlo Torlonia in Rome.

181   A dancing girl. Original model, 1837.

BUSTS

190   Ludvig Holberg. Original model, Nysø 1839.

213   Baron Hans Holsten, admiral. Original model, Nysø 1840.

215   Countess Henriette Danneskiold-Samsøe. Original model, Nysø 1839.

217   Baroness Christine Stampe. Rome 1842. Cast.

218   Ida Brun. Original model, 1810.

222   F. Siegfried Vogt, titular Councillor of State, and chargé d'affaires at Naples. Original model, 1837.

226   Adam Oehlenschläger. Original model, Nysø 1839.

227   Caspar Bartholin, Ll. B. Original model. A marble version was made in 1824; the model was made at an earlier date.

230   Jørgen Knudtzon, merchant, of Trondheim. Original model, 1816.

231   H. C. Knudtzon, merchant, of Trondheim. Original model, 1816.

238   Countess Alexandrine von Dietrichstein. Original model. Probably between 1810 and 1815.

243   Baron A. E. von Eichthal, Bavarian Court banker. Original model, 1831.

250 P incess Maria Fjodorovna Barjatinsky. Original model, 1818.

251 Countess Anna Potocka. Original model.

262 Alexander Baillie. Original model, 1816.

264A Louisa Hope, wife of Thomas Hope. Probably modelled during the winter of 1816-17. Marble (Thorvaldsen). Purchased at the Hope auction in England, 1917.

269 Countess Julia Potocka. Original model, 1833. (Formerly believed to represent a "Miss Lucan").

274 Count G. B. Sommariva. Original model, probably c. 1822-23.

277 Giovanni Raimondi Torlonia, Duke of Bracciano, Roman banker. 1829. Cast.

293 Prince Nicolaus Esterházy. Original model, 1817.

294 Henry Labouchère, later Lord Taunton, British statesman. Original model, 1828.

298 Thomas Hope. Probably modelled during the winter of 1816-17. Marble (Thorvaldsen). Purchased at the Hope auction in England, 1917.

299 George Agar Ellis, later Baron Dover. Original model, 1818.

300 Count François Gabriel de Bray. Original model, winter 1818-19.

309 Lady Harriet Frances Fleetwood Pellew. Original model, 1817.

312 The Duchess Wilhelmine of Sagan. Original model, with the curls on the forehead and temples added later. 1818. (Cf. No. 312A, p. 57).

292, 296-97, 310-11 and 313. Unidentified portrait busts. All original models.

674 Portrait of a man. Marble (Thorvaldsen).

RELIEFS

134   The genius of Poetry. Original model, 1831. Modelled for Lord Byron's statue. (Cf. No. 131, Room XIII).

339   The procession to Parnassus. Apollo with Pegasus and the genius of Light; the Graces and Muses, accompanied by cupids; Homer led by the genius of Poetry. Original model, 1832.

341   The dance of the Muses on Helicon. Modelled at Baron Schubart's villa at Villa Montenero, Leghorn, 1804, modified 1816. Original model.

347   Mercury brings the infant Bacchus to Ino. Original model, 1809.

353   Pan teaching a child satyr to play on a reed pipe. Original model, 1831.

355   A bacchante and a child satyr. Original model, 1833.

356   Pan and a hunting nymph. Original model, about 1838.

356A Pan and a hunting nymph. About 1838. Marble (Thorvaldsen).

360   Victory. Original model, about 1830. Modelled for the pedestal of the Napoleon bust, but not used.

369   Night. Original model, 1815.

370   Day. Original model, 1815.

372   Cupid feeding Hygiea's snake. Original model, 1837.

376   The Graces with Cupid in chains of roses. Original model, 1831.

381-84   Cupid's dominion over the world, or the four elements. 381: Cupid in heaven, on Jupiter's eagle, with the thunderbolt. 382: Cupid on earth, as the lion-tamer, with Hercules' club. 383: Cupid at sea on a dolphin's back, with Neptune's trident. 384: Cupid in the underworld, as the tamer of Cerberus, with a pitchfork. Original models, 1828.

385-86 Cupid on Jupiter's eagle. Original models.

387 Cupid with the tamed lion. Original model.

387A Cupid with the tamed lion. Marble.

390 Cupid riding on a lion. 1831. Cast.

392 Cupid writes the laws of Jupiter. Original model, 1831.

394 Cupid asks Jupiter that the rose may be the queen of the flowers. Original model, 1831.

400 Cupid sailing. Original model, 1831.

404 Cupid sets stone on fire. Original model, 1831.

408 Cupid with Bacchus. Original model, 1810.

411 Cupid with a swan, and boys picking fruit – Summer. Original model. Sketch made at Montenero 1810, modelled in Rome 1811.

413 Cupid and the youthful Bacchus treading grapes – Autumn. From Anacreontea, Song 17. Original model. Sketch made at Montenero 1810, modelled in Rome 1811.

415 Cupid received by Anacreon – Winter. From the Anacreontea, Song 3. 1823. Cast.

417A Cupid stung by a bee complains to Venus. Original model, 1809. Presented by the sculptor G. C. Freund, 1876.

431 Cupid revives the swooning Psyche. Original model, Montenero 1810.

433-48 Scenes from the legend of Cupid and Psyche. Modelled from Thorvaldsen's drawings in 1838 by Pietro Galli, for Palazzo Torlonia, Rome (now demolished). Casts.

455 Cupid and Hymen spinning the thread of life. Original model, 1831.

458-79 Various scenes from mythology. 458: The flight of Latona. 459: Diana with her hind. 460: Diana and

Actæon. 461, 461A: Actæon. 462-63: Diana and Orion. 464: Chione and Dædalion. 465-66: Diana and Endymion. 467-71: the nymphs of Diana. 472: Callisto. 473: Atalanta. 474: Meleager. 475: a hero with a slain lion. 476: Adonis. 477: Narcissus. 478: Apollo and Daphne. 479: Pan with the pipe Syrinx. Modelled from Thorvaldsen's drawings in 1837 by Pietro Galli for the Palazzo Torlonia, Rome (now demolished). Casts. (No. 461A: presented by G.C. Freund 1875).

483 Hylas stolen by the water-nymphs. Original model, 1831.

485 Hylas stolen by the water-nymphs. Original model, 1833.

490 Brisëis led away from Achilles by Agamemnon's heralds. The first relief made by Thorvaldsen in Rome. Original model, 1803.

492 Priam pleads with Achilles for Hector's body. Original model, 1815.

494 Achilles binds the wounds of Patroclus. Original model, 1837.

496 Achilles with the dying amazon Penthesilea. Original model, 1837.

498 Ulysses receives the arms of Achilles, awarded to him by Minerva, while Ajax departs in despair. Original model, 1831.

499 Hector with Paris and Helen. 1809. Cast.

501 Hector's farewell to Andromache. Original model, 1837.

508 FRIEZE. The Alexander procession, on a reduced scale. Made in marble in 1822 and the succeeding years by Pietro Galli.

509 Variation of the central section of the above frieze. Marble.

510-11   Parts of the original models of the Alexander procession. The trading-post by the river. A mother and
her children with the sheep.

512   Addition to the Alexander procession. A youth leading a horse. Original model, 1829.

513   Addition to the Alexander procession. A warrior
leading a horse. Original model, 1831.

515   Alexander induced by Thaïs to set fire to Persepolis.
Original model, 1832. (Cf. No. 516, p. 36).

518   Art and the light-bringing genius. "A genio lumen".
Original model, 1808.

532-45   Genii of: Poetry 532, Tragedy 533, Comedy 534,
Music 535, Dancing 536, Government 537, War 538,
Navigation 539, Trade 540, Medicine 541, Gardening
542, Agriculture 543, Astronomy 544, Religion 545.
Modelled after Thorvaldsen's drawings in 1838 by
Pietro Galli, for the Palazzo Torlonia, Rome (now
demolished). Casts.

549   Justice. Nysø 1841. Cast.

556   The Virgin and Child with John the Baptist. Original
model, 1806.

562   Christ and the two disciples at Emmaus. Original model, 1818. Made in silver for the tabernacle on the
high altar of SS. Annunziata, Florence.

565   Christ assigns the leadership of the Church to St Peter.
Original model, 1818. In marble on the front of the
altar of the chapel at Villa Poggio Imperiale, near
Florence.

571   The Virgin's flight from the Slaughter of the Innocents. Original model, 1842.

579-82   The four evangelists. Original models, 1833.

586   Angels singing. Original model, 1833.

588   Angels playing. Original model, 1833.

590-91   Hovering angels with flowers and garlands. Made
         in bronze for the high altar of Novara cathedral.
         Original models, 1833.

592   Three cupids with a garland. Original model. Cf.
         No. 649, Room XXXIV.

602   The Graces listening to Cupid's song. For the memo-
         rial to the painter Andrea Appiani, in the Brera collec-
         tion, Milan. 1821. Cast. Cf. No. 629.

626   The genius of Death. 1829. Marble. After the original
         model No. 627, p. 38.

628   Children praying. For Count Arthur Potocki's monu-
         ment in the Cathedral on Wawel Rock, Cracow. Orig-
         inal model, 1834.

629   PORTRAIT MEDALLION. The painter Andrea Appi-
         ani. Original model. Probably modelled 1821. Cf.
         No. 602.

631   —The architect Carlo (Charles) Bassi. About 1797-
         98. Cast.

632   —August von Goethe (son of the poet). Original
         model, 1831. In marble on his monument in the
         Protestant Cemetery, Rome.

633   —The philosopher Henrich Steffens. Original model,
         Nysø 1840.

635   —Portrait of a lady. Original model.

636   Thorvaldsen with the Stampe family. From left to
         right, Christian, Thorvaldsen, Jeanina, Baroness
         Stampe, and Elise. Nysø 1840. Cast.

637   Baron Stampe and his sons, Henrik (with the gun)
         and Holger (riding). Nysø 1840. Cast.

642-45   The Ages of Man and The Seasons. 642: Childhood,
         spring. 643: Youth, summer. 644: Manhood, autumn.
         645: Old age, winter. Original models, 1836.

ROOM XXII

*The ceiling coffers decorated with motifs from Roman mosaics were designed
by E. Fich, and executed by him together with William Klein and
J. J. G. Guntzelnick.*

194 BUST. Princess Vilhelmine Marie, daughter of Frederik VI. Original model, Copenhagen 1819.

261 —Lord William Bentinck, later Governor-General of India. Original model, 1816.

265 —Henry Hope, eldest son of Thomas Hope. Original model, probably modelled 1821.

266 —Younger son of Thomas Hope. Probably modelled during the winter of 1816-17. Cast.

405 RELIEF. Cupid holding out a rose, and concealing thistles. Original model, 1837.

PAINTINGS

66 *Ippolito Caffi.* A Venetian gala night.

172 *Karl Markó.* Italian mountain scene. 1836.

173 —Italian mountain scene. 1836.

176 *C. G. Plagemann.* A nun in her cell.

178 *J. C. Dahl.* The Bay of Naples by moonlight. 1821.

179 —Vesuvius in eruption. Moonlight. 1821.

180 —Grotto by the Bay of Naples. Moonlight. 1821.

181 —St Peter's Square by moonlight. 1821.

182 —Country road near La Storta. Italy. 1821.

183 —A waterfall. Italy. 1821.

184 —Norwegian mountain landscape with waterfall. 1821.

185 —Jordalsnuten, Norway. 1821.

186 —Norwegian mountain valley. 1821.

187 —The seaward approach to Copenhagen. 1830.

192 *Thomas Fearnley.* Capri viewed from Sorrento. 1833.

ROOM XXIII

The ceiling decoration is by E.Fich and William Klein, from a motif in Nero's Aurea Domus (formerly known as the Baths of Titus).

373   RELIEF. Love and Health. Hygiea crowned with a wreath by Cupid. Original model, Nysø 1840.

PAINTINGS

61   *G.B.Bassi*. Road running between garden walls (Terni). 1820.

63   —View of the ruins of the imperial palaces, Rome.

67   *Vincenzo Camuccini*. Christ blessing little children.

78   *Luigi Fioroni*. Evening scene at a Roman osteria (by Piazza della Trinità de' Monti).

79   —Pope Pius VIII carried in procession.

82   *T.Gazzarini*. The newborn Christ. 1822.

86   *M.Pacetti*. The Posilipo grotto at Naples. Copied from G.B.Bassi.

87   *P.Chauvin*. View of the garden of Villa Falconieri, Frascati. In the background Villa Rufinella (Tusculana). 1810.

88   —View of the garden of Villa d'Este, Tivoli. 1811.

89   —Grottaferrata in the Alban hills. 1811.

91   *Tancrède de la Bouère*. The coast, by the Pontine marshes. In the foreground buffaloes. 1838.

92   *Leopold Robert*. The church of San Paolo fuori le mura the day after the fire 1823. 1825.

93   —A young Greek sharpening his dagger. 1829.

ROOM XXIV

The ceiling decoration is by Ludvig Lehmann, J. J. G. Guntzelnick, and Christian Løffler, from a motif in Diomedes' villa at Pompeii.

23 STATUE. Cupid triumphant, examining his arrow. 1823. Marble (H. V. Bissen).

214 BUST. Count Conrad Danneskiold-Samsøe, Lord Lieutenant. Original model, Nordfeld 1820.

216 —Countess Louise Danneskiold-Samsøe. Original model, Gisselfeld 1820.

346 RELIEF. Mercury brings the infant Bacchus to Ino. Original model, 1809.

PAINTINGS

60 *G. B. Bassi.* Woodland scene with pool. 1816.

62 —Forest track. 1824.

84 *G. Lazzarini.* The Roman aqueduct Aqua vergine. 1823.

94 *Horace Vernet.* Half-length portrait of an Armenian priest. 1830.

98 *Filippo Agricola,* copied from Thomas Lawrence: Cardinal Ercole Consalvi.

110 *F. Catel.* A grotto in Mæcenas' villa, Tivoli.

111 —Night piece. From the closing scene of "René"; by Chateaubriand.

125 *J. A. Koch.* Apollo among the Thessalian shepherds.

128 —View of the Jungfrau from the Interlaken valley, Bernese Oberland. Figures by *J. C. Dahl.* 1821.

139 *J. C. Reinhart.* Forest scene. 1793.

140 —View of the garden of Villa Borghese.

157 *G. Schick.* Heroic landscape.

ROOM XXV

The ceiling decoration is by C.F. Sørensen, from a motif in Nero's Aurea Domus (formerly known as the Baths of Titus).

173A STATUE. Georgiana Elizabeth Russell. 1814-15. Marble (H.V. Bissen). There is a marble version in Woburn Abbey.

401   RELIEF. Cupid sailing. Original model, 1831.

PAINTINGS

109   *F. Catel.* A Neapolitan fisherman and his family.

113   *P. Cornelius.* The Entombment of Christ. 1815.

122   *A. Hopfgarten.* The miracle of St Elizabeth. 1832.

126   *J. A. Koch.* Italian landscape.

127   —Italian landscape. In the middle distance Olevano, in the Sabine hills. (On the far right is a self-portrait of the painter).

134   *E. F. Oehme.* View of a Gothic church.

135   *Moritz Oppenheim.* The return of Tobias. 1823.

136   *J. F. Overbeck.* The Virgin and Child.

141   *J. C. Reinhart.* View of Ponte Lupo near Tivoli. 1823.

143   —Italian landscape. In the foreground a hunter. 1835.

145   *H. Reinhold.* Landscape, with the Good Samaritan. 1823.

146   —Landscape, with Hagar and Ishmael. 1823.

147   —View of St Peter's from the garden of Villa Doria Pamfili. In the distance Soracte and the Sabine hills. 1823.

156   *F. W. Schadow.* The journey to Calvary.

160   *J. H. Schilbach.* View from the Capitol, looking towards the Forum. Rome 1826.

166   *T. Weller.* Street performers in the Piazza Montanara. Rome 1829.

171 *Karl Markó.* Landscape with nymphs bathing. 1834.
299 Copy after *A. J. Carstens.* The Golden Age. Figures by
     J. J. Rubbi, landscape by *F. Catel.*

ROOM XXVI

The ceiling decoration is by Magnus Petersen from a motif in Nero's Aurea
Domus (formerly known as the Baths of Titus).

37A STATUE. Hebe. 1806. Marble (Thorvaldsen). Pur-
    chased in London 1938.
264 BUST. Louisa Hope, wife of Thomas Hope. Original
     model, probably 1816-17.
228 —Madam Høyer, mother of the painter Christian
     Fædder Høyer. Original model, 1809.
345 RELIEF. Diana beseeches Jupiter for permission to de-
     vote herself to hunting. Original model, Nysø 1840.

PAINTINGS

 64 *Ippolito Caffi.* "Moccoli Evening" during the carnival
     in Rome. 1834.
161 *A. Senff.* An antique terracotta vase with flowers. 1828.
209 *C. W. Eckersberg.* Sleeping woman in antique dress.
     Alcyone's nurse. Fragment of a picture "The Dream
     of Alcyone". Ovid's Metamorphoses, XI, 410-748.
     Rome 1813.
212 —Socrates expounding a proposition to Alcibiades,
     seated naked in a chair in front of him. 1813-16.
213 —Hector's farewell to Andromache. 1813.
220 *Constantin Hansen.* View of the temple of Poseidon at
     Pæstum. 1843.
230 *J. L. Jensen.* Flowers. 1833.
231 —Fruit. 1833.
236 —White lilies and roses.

253 *J. T. Lundbye.* Landscape at Arresø, looking towards
the sand-dunes at Tisvilde. 1838. (Exhibited at the
Charlottenborg spring exhibition 1838 with this
title. Won by Thorvaldsen in the Art Society, Janu-
ary 1839. According to Johannes V. Jensen, "Arre
Sø", Hillerød 1937, the hills on the other side of the
lake are in fact the eastern shore of Auderødnæs,
with Sonnerup Wood).

254 —View from Vinderød towards Høbjerg near Frede-
riksværk, with the home of Lundbye's parents. 1839.

255 —Dolmen at Raklev, Refsnæs. May 1839.

271 *Ernst Meyer.* The courtyard of the Franciscan monastery at Amalfi.

278 *J. P. Møller.* The town of Svendborg. 1844.

282 *F. Petzholdt.* Landscape near Veii. 1835.

315 *Jens Juel.* Wilhelmine Bertouch, Lady-in-Waiting.
Pastel, presented to Thorvaldsen 1838 by the painter
Caspara Preetzmann.

ROOM XXVII

*The ceiling decoration is by A. P. Madsen, from a motif in Nero's Aurea
Domus (formerly known as the Baths of Titus).*

33 STATUE. Cupid playing on a lyre. 1819. Marble
(H. V. Bissen).

338 RELIEF. The hovering Graces. (Cf. No. 374, Room IX).
Original model, c. 1836.

PAINTINGS

197 *Wilhelm Bendz.* Artists at an evening gathering in
Finck's coffee-house, Munich. 1832.

215 *C. W. Eckersberg.* The Virgin and Child, enthroned on
the clouds. 1816.

No. 197. Wilhelm Bendz: Finck's coffee-house.

1) Wilhelm Kaulbach. 2) Heinrich Heinlein. 3) Hermann Kaufmann. 4) Marcus Haeselich. 5) Bernhard Stange. 6) Georg Heinrich Crola. 7) Karl Altmann. 8) Thomas Fearnley. 9) Andreas Borum. 10) Anton Zwengauer. 11) Eduard Schleich. 12) Heinrich Marr. 13) Philipp von Foltz. 14) Friedrich Wilhelm Vörtel. 15) Daniel Fohr. 16) Alex. Bruckmann. 17) Christen Christensen. 18) Christian Morgenstern. 19) Wilhelm Bendz. 20) Joseph Petzl.

237 *Jens Juel.* View of the Little Belt from Hindsgavl, Funen. On the left, part of Fænø. About 1800.

238 —View of the Little Belt from a hill near Middelfart. About 1800.

239 —Landscape, the Lake of Geneva (view from Veyrier towards the Jura mountains). 1777-79.

242 *J. A. Krafft.* Carnival gaiety in a Roman street. 1828.

258 *Wilhelm Marstrand.* Evening of an October Festival outside the walls of Rome. 1839.

259 *H. D. C. Martens.* The Antique Room at The Academy of fine Arts, Charlottenborg. 1824.

268 *Ernst Meyer.* A Capri fisherman.

269 —A Neapolitan fisherman at his door.

270 —A Capri fisherman.

273 —Half-length portrait of a young Franciscan.

280 *O. D. Ottesen.* Fruit. 1842.

290   *L. A. Smith.* The painter V. Gertner in his room.
292   *Jørgen Sonne.* Roman country people outside the osteria at Ponte Mammolo. 1835.
301   *J. L. Lund.* Head of a woman.

ROOM XXVIII

The ceiling decoration is by Christian Løffler, the tent motif being taken from an exedra in Nero's Aurea Domus (formerly known as the Baths of Titus).

301   BUST. Michael Coronini-Cronberg, an Austrian count. Original model, 1816. There is a marble version in Gorizia.
302   —Portrait of a boy. Original model.
555   Font. Original model (except for the garland, which is a cast), 1805–07. In marble in Brahetrolleborg church, Funen, but without the garland. Later marble versions with the garland are to be found in Reykjavik Cathedral (1827), and in the Church of the Holy Ghost, Copenhagen.

PAINTINGS

133   *F. Nerly.* Buffaloes dragging a block of marble.
150   *A. Riedel.* A Neapolitan fisherman and his family. 1833.
201   *Heinrich Buntzen.* Oaktrees by a pool. 1840.
228   *C. V. Jensen.* The manor of Gisselfeld, Zealand. 1839.
232   *J. L. Jensen.* Flowers. 1834.
246   *A. Küchler.* Roman peasants buying a hat for their little son, who is to be an "abbate". 1840.
247   —A young "abbate" recites his lesson to his sister.
249   *G. E. Libert.* View of the Sound from Langelinie. 1839.

256   *A. C. Lunde.* View of Frederiksberg Palace from the
vicinity of Ladegaardsvej.

266   *Ernst Meyer.* A Roman street letter-writer reads a letter
aloud to a young girl. 1829.

267   —The same, writing a letter for the girl.

276   *Adam Müller.* Christ and the Evangelists. 1842.

279   *Hermania Neergaard.* Flowers. 1842.

284   *F. Richardt.* A studio at the Academy of Fine Arts,
Charlottenborg.

286   *M. Rørbye.* View of Athens from the south-west.
Athens, 1836.

291   *Jørgen Sonne.* A battlefield on the morning after the
battle. 1833.

298   *F. Thøming.* Breakers on the coast of Capri.

ROOM XXIX

*The ceiling decoration is by Heinrich Hansen, from a motif in Nero's
Aurea Domus (formerly known as the Baths of Titus).*

35   STATUE. Cupid standing with his bow. Marble
(Thorvaldsen). Purchased in 1914 at the sale of the
effects of Dr Carl Jacobsen of the Carlsberg Breweries.

PAINTINGS

58   *Antonio Aquaroni.* Ponte Cestio. 1836.

68   *Alessandro Castelli.* Landscape.

101   *Penry Williams.* A shepherd-boy and a girl in the
Roman Campagna. 1842.

138   *J. Rebell.* The Isle of Capri. 1820.

162   *J. Steingrübel.* View of Florence. 1834.

177   *J. C. Dahl.* The Bay of Naples by moonlight. 1821.

198   *Ditlev Blunck.* Noah in the Ark. 1835.

202   *Heinrich Buntzen.* The so-called villa of Raphael in the garden of the Villa Borghese. 1843.

219   *F. Nordahl Grove.* View from Baunbjerg by Horsens Fjord. 1842.

233   *J. L. Jensen.* Still life. 1835.

234   —Flowers. 1838.

243   *A. Küchler.* The death of Correggio. 1834.

244   —Domestic scene by Lake Nemi. 1837.

263   *Anton Melbye.* A calm morning at sea. 1840.

277   *J. P. Møller.* Svendborg Sound. 1843.

293   *F. Thøming.* A Danish corvette.

296   —View of the coast of Capri. 1829.

ROOM XXX

The ceiling decoration is by C. Weber from a motif in Nero's Aurea Domus (formerly known as the Baths of Titus).

244   BUST. Frau von Krause, wife of Jacob von Krause, Austrian consul-general in St Petersburg. Original model, 1819.

282   —The painter Vincenzo Camuccini. Original model, 1810.

314   —Portrait of a child. Cast.

315   —Portrait of a child, possibly Georgiana Elizabeth Russell and a preliminary study for the statue No. 173 (corridor, first floor).

126   SKETCH MODEL. Prince Jozef Poniatowski. Original model.

PAINTINGS

74   *F. Diofebi.* The approach to the Villa Borghese. 1838.

100   *Joseph Severn.* Vintage scene. 1828.

104 *M. Verstappen.* A roadside chapel between Albano and
      Ariccia.
119 *A. Henning.* Half-length portrait of the model Fortunata.
120 *G. E. Hering.* A street in Smyrna. 1835.
151 *A. Riedel.* Girl bathing. 1837.
164 *C. W. Tischbein.* Neapolitan fisherman's daughter.
165 *E. Wächter.* The painter Joseph Anton Koch.
170 *Karl Markó.* Nymphs bathing. 1834.
190 *Thomas Fearnley.* Norwegian landscape. 1833.
208 *Dankvart Dreyer.* View of the coast near Aarhus. Ex-
      hibited 1839.
241 *F. T. Kloss.* Approach to Copenhagen by sea. 1838.
251 *J. L. Lund.* St Anne teaching the Virgin to read. 1818.

ROOM XXXI

*The ceiling decoration is by A. J. C. Riise from a motif in the Villa of
Diomedes in Pompeii.*

 25 STATUE. Psyche with the jar of beauty. 1806. Marble
      (Thorvaldsen). Purchased at the Hope auction in
      England, 1917.
432 RELIEF. Psyche taken up to heaven by Mercury.
      Original model.

PAINTINGS

 65 *Ippolito Caffi.* La Girandola fireworks during the
      Easter celebrations in Rome.
 72 *F. Diofebi.* St Joseph's Day in Rome. 1832.
 73 —The opening of Raphael's grave in 1833, on which
      occasion Thorvaldsen represented the Accademia
      di San Luca, Rome. 1836.
 80 *Beniamino de Francesco.* Italian landscape. 1836.
 95 *Horace Vernet.* Thorvaldsen. 1835.

No. 199. Ditlev Blunck: Danish artists at the osteria
La Gensola.

1) Albert Küchler. 2) Waiter. 3) M.G.Bindesbøll. 4) Wilhelm Marstrand. 5) Constantin Hansen. 6) Jørgen Sonne. 7) Ditlev Blunck. 8) Ernst Meyer. 9) Thorvaldsen.

105A *Friedrich von Amerling.* Thorvaldsen. (c. 1841-42). Purchased 1929.

148 *J.Richter.* The model Fortunata. 1833.

149 —Roman woman. 1834.

163A *R.Suhrlandt.* Thorvaldsen. 1810. Presented 1921 by the family of Oscar Gad the publisher.

164A *Vogel von Vogelstein.* Thorvaldsen. 1814. Purchased 1890.

199 *Ditlev Blunck.* Danish artists at the osteria La Gensola, Rome. 1837.

217 *C.W.Eckersberg.* Thorvaldsen's arrival in the Copenhagen roadstead, September 17th 1838. 1839.

258C *Wilhelm Marstrand.* M.G.Bindesbøll the architect. 1844. Bequeathed to the Royal Museum of Fine Arts, Copenhagen, by Miss Karen Johanne Bindesbøll; deposited in Thorvaldsen's Museum 1935.

281   *O.D. Ottesen.* A luncheon table. 1844.
285   *F. Richardt.* Thorvaldsen in his studio at the Academy
      of Fine Arts, Charlottenborg. 1840.
287   *M. Rørbye.* Harbour scene, Palermo. 1844.
295   *F. Thøming.* The Bay of Naples. Thorvaldsen and
      Thøming are seated in the nearest fishing-boat, with
      other travellers. 1828.

*   *   *

The *showcases* contain personal relics of Thorvaldsen, including his medals, watches, rings, and flute, his self-portrait
of 1794, J. A. Jerichau's portrait of Anna Maria Magnani, the
portrait of Miss Frances Mackenzie drawn by Thorvaldsen,
his decorations, the document of 1838 giving him the free-
dom of Copenhagen, and his little collection of oriental
bronze bowls. These are Islamic work of the 14th and 15th
centuries, made in Egypt or Syria, with the exception of
two which were made in Venice by Persians.

ROOM XXXII

*The ceiling decoration is by G. C. Hilker, from a motif in Nero's Aurea
Domus (formerly known as the Baths of Titus). It was executed in 1843,
and was the first of these decorations.*

THORVALDSEN'S LAST UNFINISHED WORKS

188   Bust of Martin Luther. Original model, Copenhagen
      1844.
524   Chalk sketch on a slate for the relief showing the
      genius of Sculpture seated on the shoulder of the
      statue of Jupiter. Copenhagen 1844.

OTHER WORKS BY THORVALDSEN

Clock-case carved by Thorvaldsen in his youth. Presented in 1860 by C. A. Ollendorff, Holbæk.

425 RELIEF. Shepherdess with a nest of cupids. Original model, 1831.

598 —Christian charity. Original model, 1810.

630 PORTRAIT MEDALLION. E. H. Løffler, drawing-master at the Academy of Fine Arts. Copenhagen 1796. Cast.

634 —The painter Heinrich Reinhold. Original model, 1825. Marble version on Reinhold's monument in the Protestant Cemetery in Rome.

PAINTINGS

108 *C. G. Carus.* A prehistoric barrow by moonlight.

112 *F. Catel.* Landscape at sunset.

129 *J. A. Koch.* Noah's sacrifice after the Flood. 1815.

160A *Louise Seidler.* Fanny Caspers. 1819. Bequeathed in 1937 by Dr Rudolf von Stankiewicz, Vienna.

163 *J. Stieler.* King Ludwig I of Bavaria.

168 *A. Koop.* Copy of K. Begas' portrait of Thorvaldsen (1823). 1828.

188 *J. C. Dahl.* The coast at Laurvig, Norway 1840.

189 —From Øvre Telemark, Norway 1840.

191 *Thomas Fearnley.* The sea at Palermo. 1833.

199A *Ditlev Blunck.* Two German doctors, Dr Karl von Pfeuffer and Dr Geist, who lived in the same house as Thorvaldsen during the cholera epidemic in Rome in 1837.

203 *Heinrich Buntzen.* Nysø. 1843.

207 *C. Dahl.* Larsens Plads, Copenhagen. 1840.

210 *C. W. Eckersberg.* A harvester in antique dress. 1813-16.

211 —A Roman beggar. 1815.

214   *C. W. Eckersberg*. St Peter's Square, Rome. 1813–16.
216   —Frederik VI. 1839. Replica of a painting made in 1820.
217A —The Colosseum, Rome. 1813–16.
220A *Constantin Hansen*. M.G.Bindesbøll, builder of the Museum. 1849. Commissioned by the directors of the Museum.
220C —View of Thorvaldsen's Museum. 1858. Presented in 1938 by C.B.Henriques.
227   *C. A. Jensen*. The flower painter C. D. Fritzsch. (c. 1835?).
227A —Baroness Christine Stampe. 1827. Presented in 1924 by the Barony of Stampenborg.
227B —Thorvaldsen. 1839. Presented in 1926 by Prince and Princess Murat.
227C —The writer Ludvig Bødtcher. 1836. Presented in 1942 by Mrs Elisabeth Theodor Jensen.
245   *A. Küchler*. Colonel and Mrs Paulsen, Thorvaldsen's son-in-law and daughter, with their two children. 1838.
258B *Wilhelm Marstrand*. Just Mathias Thiele, Thorvaldsen's biographer. Purchased 1874.
265   *Anton Melbye*. Fishing-boats in the Channel. 1844.
272   *Ernst Meyer*. A Franciscan monk.

*   *   *

The furniture with tapestry seats and backs is from Thorvaldsen's residence at Charlottenborg; it was presented to him by a circle of Copenhagen ladies on his "Roman birthday", March 8th 1840.

ROOM XXXIII

The ceiling decoration is by G. C. Hilker, from a motif in Nero's Aurea Domus (formerly known as the Baths of Titus).

SKETCH MODELS

FOR STATUES AND MONUMENTS

13A Venus and Cupid. Cast. Lent by the Hirschsprung Collection, Copenhagen, 1932.

19A Nemesis. Original model.

49-50 A triumphant Muse. Original models, 1827.

57-58 Sibyl. Original models.

73-81 Figures for the Preaching of John the Baptist. Original models (cf. Nos. 59-70, p. 32).

84-85 Christ. Original models.

88-109 The apostles. 88: Matthew. 90: John. 92: James the Less. 97: Thomas. 100: Bartholomew. 102: Simon Zelotes. 104: Paul. 106-107: Thaddæus. 109: Andrew. Original models.

111 and 112A. Angel holding a font. Original models. (112A: Baked clay. Bequeathed in 1876 by Johan Bravo).

157 The genii of Life and Death. Original model.

158 The genii of Life and Death beside a meta. Original model.

159 Kneeling angel. Original model, Nysø 1839.

175 Boy hunter. Thorvaldsen's grandson Alberto Paulsen. Original model, Nysø 1843.

177A Shepherd-boy. Original model. Purchased 1854 from the Buti family, Rome.

178A Dancer. Original model. Purchased 1875.

182 Young girl dancing. Original model.

184 Flower-girl. Original model.

185 Youth with a dog. Original model.

SKETCH MODELS FOR RELIEFS

118 The invention of the printing-press. Original model.

153 Three genii. The motto of Christian IV: *Regna firmat pietas*. Like statue No. 152 (Room XXI), originally intended for the monument to Christian IV in Roskilde Cathedral. Original model, Nysø 1842.

344 Apollo among the shepherds. 1837. Cast.

427 The Ages of Love. 1824. Retouched in Copenhagen, 1843. Cast.

546-47 The genii of the Arts and Trades. Modelled by Pietro Galli in 1838 from Thorvaldsen's drawings, for the Palazzo Torlonia in Rome (now demolished). Casts.

552 Adam and Eve with Cain and Abel. Original model. Cf. No. 551, p. 36.

554 The judgment of Solomon. Original model, 1835. Sketch model for a pediment for the Law Courts in Copenhagen.

561 The Resurrection of Christ. 1835. Sketch model for a pediment for the Palace chapel. Cast.

566 Christ blessing the children. Nysø 1839. Cast.

604 The abolition of villeinage. Original model, Copenhagen 1842. Sketch model for Frederik VI's monument at Skanderborg. Cf. No. 605-10.

605 The establishment of provincial consultative chambers. Original model, Copenhagen, winter 1842-43. Cf. No. 604.

606 The rule of Justice. Original model, Copenhagen 1843. Cf. No. 604.

607 The protection of the Arts and Sciences. Original model, Copenhagen, winter 1842-43. Cf. No. 604.

609 Justice and Strength. Original model, Copenhagen
     1843. Cf. No. 604.

617 Sketch model for the memorial to the young Ponin-
     skis. Original model, 1835. Cf. No. 616, p. 37.

ROOM XXXIV

*The ceiling decoration is by David Jacobsen and M. M. Goldschmidt,
from a motif in Hadrian's villa.*

649 Marble chimney-piece with two caryatids and a frieze
     of cupids. (Cf. the original model No. 592, p. 64).
     Marble (Thorvaldsen).

SKETCH MODELS FOR RELIEFS

349-350 The abduction of Ganymede. Original models,
         1833.

449 Cupid and Psyche. "Goodbye to Nysø". Nysø 24th
     May 1841. Cast.

453 Cupid garlands Hymen's torches. Original model,
     Copenhagen 1840.

550 Denmark praying for the king. Original model, Co-
     penhagen 1839, for a medal on the occasion of the
     accession of Christian VIII.

574 Christ's entry into Jerusalem. Original model, 1842.

608 The abolition of villeinage. For the Skanderborg
     monument to Frederik VI. Copenhagen 1842. Cast.
     Cf. No. 604 (p. 83).

610 Genii strewing flowers on the symbols of the Arts and
     Sciences. For the Skanderborg monument to Frede-
     rik VI. Original model, Copenhagen 1843. Cf. No.
     607 (p. 83).

648 Bacchante with a bird. Original model, 1837.

SKETCH MODELS
FOR STATUES AND MONUMENTS

5 A Mercury about to kill Argus. Original model. Purchased 1931.

10 Vulcan. Original model.

15-16 Hercules. Original models.

17-18 Minerva. Original models.

19 Nemesis. Original model.

20-21 Æsculapius. Original models.

15-21 are sketch models for the four colossal statues in Prince Jørgen's Courtyard at Christiansborg Palace, of which Thorvaldsen lived to complete only Hercules (cf. No. 14, p. 37), the rest being executed after his death by H. V. Bissen on the basis of his sketches. Modelled in Copenhagen 1839.

30 The Graces. Original model.

48 Victory. Original model.

113 A Copernicus. Original model. Presented in 1922 by Marius Nielsen.

117 Gutenberg. Original model. Modelled in Rome 1833 by H. V. Bissen under Thorvaldsen's direction.

120 Monument to General, Prince Schwarzenberg. Original model, 1821.

133 Lord Byron. Original model.

138 Schiller. 1835. Cast.

139 Goethe. Copenhagen, probably 1839. Cast.

140 Goethe. Original model, Copenhagen, probably spring 1840.

141 Frederik VI. Original model, Copenhagen 1840.

148-49 Monument to Pope Pius VII in St Peter's, Rome. Original models.

151 Conradin, the last of the Hohenstaufens. Original model.

160-61   Luther and Melanchthon. Original models. Statues
         for the Church of Our Lady, Copenhagen; not exe-
         cuted.

163   Thorvaldsen's self-portrait statue (cf. No. 162A,
         Room xx). Nysø 1839. Cast.

168-69   Seated lady. Original models.

170   Seated lady with a boy. Original model.

ROOM XXXV

*The motif of the ceiling decoration is taken from the Villa of Diomedes
in Pompeii, and was executed by J.F.Busch and Magnus Petersen.*

EGYPTIAN ANTIQUITIES

Most of these were found in tombs where they adorned
the mummy or otherwise served as burial equipment. Some
of the objects had been used in life, and were buried with
the dead in order that they might be used again in the next
world. The earliest period of Egyptian civilization is not
represented in the collection, the greater part of which is
from the late Egyptian period (c. 600 B. C.-A. D. 300), while
a few objects are from c. 1600-1000 B. C.

Cabinet 1. The three top rows contain representations of
gods. The smallest are amulets, the largest served various
religious purposes, such as votive offerings. The fourth row
of this cabinet, and the top row of showcase 2 contain
images of sacred animals which were objects of worship
and religious cults.

Cases 2-3. Amulets and seals; the latter have a flat under
surface with signs and figures incised (impressions in plaster
attached). The commonest form is the scarab, imitating the
shape of the sacred chafer. The material is in most cases a
soft stone (steatite), or the so-called Egyptian earthenware.

The under surface has incised pictures of gods, kings, sacred animals, hieroglyphics containing the names of gods and kings (especially that of the great pharaoh Thotmes III), or various signs for bringing luck and warding off evil.

Cabinet 4. Pots, cups, and vases, mainly of alabaster. Nos. 282-301 were used for ointments and cosmetics; the inscription on No. 301 shows that it was a New Year's gift.

Case 5. Rings, those of bronze and silver being seal-rings. Beads, some of which were placed in a network on mummies, or formed a necklace; some of the beads and the mounted scarabs undoubtedly come from Italian burial finds.

Case 6. Nos. 251-252, handles of a musical instrument (sistrum) used in the worship of Isis. Nos. 253-254, small vessels used for religious purposes. No. 256, a case containing black kohl, and the stick for applying it. No. 257, a bronze mirror.

Cabinet 7 and the two adjoining cases contain burial deposits. The stones Nos. 345-349 and the wooden tablet No. 350 show the dead sacrificing to various gods, or being themselves venerated by their families, with hieroglyphic inscriptions giving names, titles, and religious formulas. The figures Nos. 361-381, usually found in large numbers in the grave enclosed in a wooden chest, were placed there, according to inscriptions, in order that they might work in the fields for the dead man in the next world.

Cases 8-9. Mummy ornaments. Nos. 394-97, breast-ornaments made of cloth covered with stucco and painted or gilded. Nos. 398-400, breast-plates of earthenware, painted wood, and talc. Nos. 402-11, scarabs placed upon the breast of the dead.

Below: Burial urns, "canopic vases", which contained the viscera, separately embalmed; they are found, in sets of

four, placed beside the mummy in a separate coffin. The lids are formed like the heads of a man, a monkey, a jackal, and a hawk, symbolizing the four divine beings believed to protect the embalmed body.

Plaster casts of two statues of Egyptian kings (No. 1, Meneptah III, No. 2, Amenophis III), and of the lid of a mummy sarcophagus (No. 3).

Books from Thorvaldsen's library.

ROOM XXXVI

The ceiling decoration is by Heinrich Hansen from a motif in Nero's Aurea Domus (formerly known as the Baths of Titus). The central picture is by T. Wegener.

GREEK, ETRUSCAN, AND ROMAN ANTIQUITIES

Cabinet 1. Bronze figures. Nos. 1–23, 25–28 *Etruscan.* 2, a goddess. 5, a youthful and beardless Jupiter. 6, Minerva. 8–10, Sileni. 16–19, athletes. 27–28, lion-heads, possibly grave ornaments. Nos. 24, 29, 32–82 *Greek and Roman.* 32, Athene. 33, Cybele and Attis. 34, Jupiter. 36, Ceres. 38, Apollo. 40, Mars. 41, Venus. 44–46, Mercury. 47, Silenus. 48–49, Priapus. 50, Telesphorus. Phallic figure, covered by a cape. 51–55, Cupid. 61, Telamon. 62–65, sacrificing Lar (the god of the household). 69, Hercules. 75, an actor. The figures of gods were placed in private houses, or were votive offerings to temples; the remaining figures were part of the ornamentation of vessels and other objects.

Cases 2–3. Figures, heads, masks etc., of bronze, most of them originally decorations on vessels or other furniture. No. 29, two lions attacking a hind, Tarentum, 4th centuri B. C.

Cabinet 4. Etruscan bronze mirrors. The front was originally polished to serve as a mirror; the back is engraved with
motifs from ancient myths.

Case 5. Rings, amulet-lockets, buckles, necklets and arm-
rings, hairpins, etc. of bronze.

Case 6. Various small objects, balances and weights, tokens, keys, spoons, surgical instruments and forceps, bath
scrapers (Nos. 357-58), etc., of bronze.

Cabinet 7. Ladles, pitchers, dishes, and bowls for practical
or religious use (Nos. 230-68); lamps (Nos. 304-05); a can-
delabrum for four lamps, Etruria, about 400 B. C. (No.
306); feet and mounts of various pieces of furniture (Nos.
308-28); bells (No. 348-50); bath scrapers (No. 356, 359);
various other tools and weapons (Nos. 369-87).

Cabinet 8. Vessels for ordinary use, including strainers
(Nos. 259-262); vases for ointment (Nos. 269-71); handles
of various kinds of vessels (Nos. 272-300. No. 273 represents
a young man and two lions, South Italic-Greek, middle of
the 6th century B. C.; No. 283 represents Scylla, Tarentum,
end of the 4th or beginning of the 3rd century B. C.); the
feet of vessels (Nos. 301-02); knife hilt in the form of an
ornamental table-leg (No. 303); arrowheads (Nos. 378-79);
spear- and lance-heads (No. 374-76); tip of a lance (No.
377); axes (palstaves) (Nos. 369-70).

Case 9. Ivory and bone objects. No. 22, piece used in
some game. No. 23, a so-called gladiator-token. No. 25, a
doll, probably from the Catacombs in Rome. Nos. 3-8
and 10 are from Etruscan graves.

Case 10. II. Ornaments and amulets (Nos. 102-12), fragments of vases (Nos.117-22), of chalcedony, carnelian,
crystal, and other more precious stones. IV. Nos. 3-12, silver
amulets and ornaments; No. 4, arrow-head of flint mounted
in silver. VI. Objects made of lead. Nos. 20-78 are tokens

used for plays, baths, corn-distribution, or for other purposes.

Cabinet 11. Nos. 1-68. A pitcher, oil-flasks, etc., made of
glass. Those made of fused glass in different colours are of
Egyptian technique. No. 1, millefiori bowl. Nos. 91-94,
glass mosaic cubes. IV, 1. A Roman silver portrait head of
the emperor Antoninus Pius (A. D. 138-161). VIII, 1. An
ivory head of Jupiter Serapis (cf. the marble statue No. 2,
Room xxxix, Cabinet 1).

Case 12. Glass. Nos. 28-30, fragments of bowls with
white raised figures. Nos. 37-42, fragments of handles. Nos.
69-90, fragments of ornaments from walls and ceilings.
Nos. 95-126, imitations of precious stones, beads, and links
of necklets.

Case 13. Gold ornaments, mostly from Etruscan graves.
Nos. 1-16, rings; on the discs of the first three are animal
figures in early Etruscan style. Nos. 17-44, ear ornaments.
No. 45, necklet. Nos. 46-54, beads etc. of necklets or ear
ornaments. Nos. 55-62, amulet-lockets and amulets (No. 61
contains a flint arrow-head, No. 62 a fossilized shark's tooth).
No. 64, arm-ring. Nos. 65-75, various ornaments to be
worn on the clothing (Nos. 66 and 67 were made for burial
equipment; Nos. 68-74 are probably ear ornaments).

Books from Thorvaldsen's library.

ROOM XXXVII

*In the ceiling decoration, the Bacchus is by T. Wegener. The rest is by
Philip August Fischer, from a motif in Nero's Aurea Domus (formerly
known as the Baths of Titus).*

WORKS BY THORVALDSEN

226B BUST. Portrait of a man. Original model. (Formerly
    believed to represent Georg Zoëga). Purchased 1898.

240D BUST. The writer Elisa von der Recke. Half size. Original model, probably winter 1805-06. Purchased 1944.

279A —The *improvisatrice* R. Taddei. Original model, 1826.

280A —The architect J. L. Thrane. Original model, c. 1805-06.

ANTIQUE GEMS AND PASTES

The showcases in this room, like those in Rooms XXXVI, XXXVIII, XXXIX, and XL, were designed by the Museum architect, M. G. Bindesbøll.

The cases contain cut, precious or hard stones *(gems)*, and glass imitations of these *(pastes)*, dating from antiquity.

The gems are displayed according to the original arrangement made by the first keeper of the museum, the numismatist Ludvig Müller, with the original leather labels. The numbers of the gems and pastes are written on the sides of the plaster impressions arranged in rows below the stones. The numbers begin in the case facing Room XXXVIII, nearest the window.

Gems and pastes were used as seals, and were generally worn in rings. The gold rings Nos. 2, 40, 44, 56, 388, 661, 1053 are antique; the remaining gold rings are modern. Nos. 142, 144, 206, 291, 326, 372, 402, 615, 653, 1618, and others, have retained part of their antique setting in rings of silver, bronze, or iron. The designs on the gems, which cover a wide range of motifs, are presumably seal marks, and the occasional inscriptions give the name or initials of the owner.

Nos. 1-59, marked "Scarabs", are shaped like the sacred chafer, an originally Egyptian form, found particularly in Etruria. Nos. 1-44 are Etruscan, Nos. 53-59 Graeco-Roman.

Nos. 60-81, marked "Early Style", i. e. the archaic style, are from Greece and Etruria.

Nos. 82-1583, marked "Developed Art", i. e. the classical
and Hellenistic styles, are from Greece and Rome. The gems
are arranged in the following groups, according to their
motifs: gods, heroes, historical episodes, human occupations,
animals, and symbolical groups.

Nos. 1584-1693, marked "The Decline of Art", i. e. the
late classical style. Nos. 1678-93 belong to the so-called
Abraxas stones, the designs and inscriptions on which derive
from the religious mysteries and from the mixture of reli-
gions found in the 2nd to the 5th centuries after Christ,
especially in Syria and Egypt. They were religious symbols
and amulets used by the gnostics and other sects.

Gems and pastes with raised figures are known as *cameos*
(Nos. 1-129). They were used as personal ornaments (No.
72 is set in an antique gold ring), and as decorations, for instance for caskets and vases.

*   *   *

Casts of antique reliefs are set in the walls.

Nos. 275-76, racing chariots. Neo-Attic, 1st century B.C.
The originals are privately owned in Portugal.

No. 278, three city goddesses. Formerly in the Villa
Borghese, now in storage in the Louvre. Probably not
genuine.

Drawings, in the wall-frames:

No. 1. *A.J. Carstens:* Night with her children Sleep and
Death. Black and white crayon. Copy by *Thorvaldsen.*

No. 332. *A.J. Carstens:* Megapenthes is brought to Charon's boat. Water-colour. Copy by *J.A. Koch.*

No. 333. *A.J. Carstens:* Megapenthes crossing the Styx in
Charon's boat. Water-colour. Copy by *J.A. Koch.*

No. 334. *A.J. Carstens:* Agathon's feast. Water-colour.
1793.

ROOM XXXVIII

The ceiling decoration is by Joel Ballin and C. Weber, from a motif in Nero's Aurea Domus (formerly known as the Baths of Titus).

ANTIQUE COINS

I. Greek coins. A. Before the middle of the 5th century B. C. Archaic style. The coins in this section are all silver; gold coins of this period are comparatively rare, and copper (bronze) was not yet minted. Some, the earliest, are struck on one side only, and the majority have no inscription, or merely the initials of a people or a town. Nos. 1-14, which were coined on the island of Aegina, are the oldest in the collection, belonging to the 7th century B. C. *B. From the middle of the 5th century B. C. to the Roman empire.* Classical and Hellenistic style. During this period copper coins were in general use, and gold coins were minted more frequently. The coins are flatter, rounder, and (with few exceptions) struck on both sides. Many of these coins are of high artistic quality, e. g. those from Sicyon, Corinth, Elis, Focis, Locris, and Macedonia, and especially those from southern Italy and Sicily. The inscriptions are longer, and more varied; the names of kings and magistrates now also occur. *C. The period of the Roman empire.* Silver was minted more rarely by the dependent Greek cities and princes, and gold only in exceptional cases. The coins generally bear the head and name of the emperor on one side and, like those of the preceding sections, have Greek inscriptions.

II. Coins of other nations. Of the *Persian* coins, the first four are from the time of the Achæmenids, the kings before Alexander the Great's conquest; the next eight are from the Arsacidean dynasty, and the last two from the time of the Sassanidæ. The gold and silver coins displayed in the *Phoenician* group were struck by the Carthaginians after the conquest of Sicily, whose Greek coins they resemble; some of them derive from Greek die-cutters, but the inscriptions are Phoenician. The coins struck in Spain by the *Celtiberi* are from the second and first centuries B. C. The designs show the influence of Roman stamping; the inscriptions are Celtiberian. The coins of the *Italic* peoples are partly cast, made of copper and of a good weight, partly struck, like the Greek coins of southern Italy, from which they often differ only in the inscriptions, which are Etruscan, Umbrian, and Oscan. They belong to the period between the 4th and 2nd centuries B. C. The last row contains coins of *barbarian* nations in Gaul and Pannonia, imitating the Greek and Roman.

III. Coins of Roman colonies. A. The time of the republic. These commonly have the stamp formerly used in the cities and provinces where they have been struck; but the inscriptions are in Latin, and the name of Rome, or the names and portraits of Roman rulers, testify to Roman domination. *B. The time of the empire.* These coins, whose inscriptions are likewise in Latin, generally have the head and name of the emperor or empress on the obverse, and on the reverse the distinguishing stamp of the different countries and cities.

IV. Roman coins. A. During the republic. The earliest (top row) were of bronze, and cast, namely the *as* and its subdivisions, which were denoted by various heads of gods, and marks; later they were struck (second row). Silver coins, of which the denarius was the most common, were first struck shortly before the First Punic War. The designs and inscriptions change constantly since it was left to the authorities in charge of the minting to choose the stamp. *B. The time of the empire.* The obverse generally displays the head of the emperor or empress, or some other member of the imperial family, with name and title, while the designs on the reverse vary.

V. Byzantine coins, struck by the emperors of the Eastern Empire. The first still have the Roman stamp; the next have Christian symbols and pictures, and on the last the inscriptions are in Greek.

MEDALLIONS

The case under the window. Medallions Nos. 15-25 display reproductions of works by Thorvaldsen. Nos. 26-31 and 131 are by medallists before Thorvaldsen's time, and Nos. 36-130 and 132-135 are by medallists who were his contemporaries.

PAINTINGS

1 *Lorenzo Monaco,* Florence, early 15th century. The Virgin and Child.

2 *Taddeo di Bartolo,* Siena, about 1400. Predella showing Christ in Gethsemane, the Crucifixion, the Resurrection, Mary Magdalen, and St Catherine.

3 *Florentine,* 15th century. The Virgin and Child. Copy, with variations, of a painting by *A.Baldovinetti* in the National Gallery, Washington.

4 *Fiorenzo di Lorenzo,* Umbria, late 15th century. Two panels from an altar-piece, showing St Eligius and St John the Baptist.

5 Virgin and Child. Copy of a painting by *Pinturicchio* in the National Gallery, Washington.

10 *Francesco Bassano the Younger* (attributed to), Venice, late 16th century. "Domestic evening tasks".

16 *Giovanni Battista Salvi,* called *Sassoferrato,* Rome, 17th century. Praying Virgin.

20 *Giovanni Francesco Barbieri,* called *Guercino,* Bologna, 17th century. Young girl reading.

44 *Pieter Brueghel the Younger*, known as Hell Brueghel
     (attributed to), the Netherlands, 16th-17th century.
     Hell.
50 *Dutch*, 17th-18th century. Landscape in the style of
     G. Dughet. Possibly by *J. F. van Bloemen*.

On the cabinet at the back, which contains the rest of the
collection of antique coins, is a marble bust of Thorvaldsen
by an unknown artist (original model 1812).

ROOM XXXIX

*The central picture of the ceiling decoration – Psyche imploring Venus –
is by Thomas Wegener. The rest is by C. F. Sørensen, from a motif in
Nero's Aurea Domus (formerly known as the Baths of Titus).*

ANTIQUE SCULPTURES IN MARBLE,
TERRACOTTA, ETC.

Left wall. Mainly Roman marbles. On the *brackets:* No. 7
Mercury, head, Roman copy of a Greek original of the
4th century B. C.; 13-14, heads of satyrs; 24, head of a
Pudicitia-statue (limestone); 29, torso of a young man; 37,
the emperor Hadrian apotheosized (marble work of the
18th century); 39, portrait head of the emperor Septimius
Severus, 2nd-3rd century; 40, portrait head, end of 1st century, with pieces of stone attached in preparation for a restoration; 41, alabaster portrait bust, probably representing
one of the twelve Suetonian emperors, Italy, about 1600;
47, female portrait, second half of the 2nd century; 69,
fragment of a Roman portrait of a boy, second half of the
2nd century; 82, fragment of the pedestal of a marble table,
middle of the 2nd century B. C.; 83-84, architectural fragments with sculpture on both sides, on No. 83 the head of

a Cyclops. *Let into the wall:* No. 76, fragment of a Greek votive relief to Asklepios (Æsculapius), 4th century B. C.; 77, monkey eating a root, fragment of an architectural panel in relief; 90, fragment of a Greek tomb relief, showing a scene of parting, 4th century B. C. *At the foot of the wall:* No. 5, right leg of an Apollo statue, with a griffin, showing traces of red colouring; 18, head of Pan; 92, burial urn.

Cabinet 1. Mainly Roman marbles. No. 1, Cybele; 4, Minerva, copy of a Greek work of about 450 B. C.; 6, Ephesian Artemis (Diana); 11, Bacchus; 12, Mercury, Roman work in archaistic style; 20-22, Æsculapius; 25, woman's head in basalt, 1st century; 28, statuette torso in calc-spar, representing the city goddess of Antioch, a Roman reproduction of the original statue by *Eutychides* (3rd century B. C.); 32, torso of a statuette of Jupiter Serapis, inspired by the colossal statue by *Bryaxis* in Alexandria (4th century B. C.); 34, head of a youth, Roman work in the style of *Polycleitus;* 45, head of a Roman woman, possibly the empress Domitia, polished quartz, 1st century; 50, fragment of the statue of an athlete, known as Diadumenos, Roman copy of an original by *Polycleitus* (5th century B. C.); 67, Cybele in a naiscos (small temple), Greek original work, 4th century B. C.; 74, relief showing Diana; 91, Roman portrait head, probably a sarcophagus relief, 3rd century. *On top of the cabinet:* No. 35, head of a youth, Roman copy of an original in the style of *Polycleitus;* 36, head of a statue of Demosthenes, Roman copy of an original by *Polyeuctus* (3rd century B. C.); 48, late Roman portrait of a boy, 2nd-3rd century.

Cabinet 2. Terracotta. Figures and heads of the type of Nos. 1-13 and 26-34 were chiefly used as burial gifts and votive offerings. The burial gifts were buried with the dead,

the offerings were kept in the shrines. Some of them represent goddesses, others, such as the Italic heads Nos. 6-10,
persons placed under the protection of the gods. The enthroned goddesses Nos. 1-3 are in archaic Greek style. The
draped female figures Nos. 18-24 were displayed as ornaments in the home, and then buried in the grave. Nos. 6-
13 and 44 are Etrusco-Italic. All the remaining figures come
from the Greek colonies in southern Italy; Nos. 26, 28-29,
and 31-34 are probably from Paestum. No. 263 is a little
Etrusco-Italic altar, Nos. 264-66 Roman lamp-stands.

Right wall. Terracotta. On the *bracket:* Antefixes and
waterspouts, including three in the shape of actors' masks
(Nos. 53-55). *Let into the wall:* Fragments of friezes from the
walls of temples, houses, and tombs, presumably found in
the neighbourhood of Rome. Most of them are Roman,
Greek-inspired; a few (such as the temple servants Nos. 65-
66 and the Gorgon masks Nos. 120-123) are archaistic. *Below the showcase:* three large frieze panels showing the La-
bours of Hercules (Nos. 96-98).

Cases 3-4. Roman clay lamps from the time of the empire.
Nos. 249 and 250 are from the period after the acceptance
of Christianity; Nos. 256-62 are miniature copies for
burial use.

Case 5. Figures and heads, some of which are fragments
of larger objects, some toys (Nos. 47-50 are possibly Greek),
masks once decorating chests (Nos. 270-71 are Etruscan,
from Campania), vessels, and lamps; fragments of red Ar-
retine pottery, etc.

On the *window wall,* a marble figure in relief (Apollo;
No. 71), and a Roman mosaic (battle-scene; believed to be
a fake; No. 97).

ROOM XL

The ceiling decoration is by C.F. Sørensen, from a motif in Nero's Aurea Domus (formerly known as the Baths of Titus).

GREEK, ITALIC, AND ETRUSCAN POTTERY

Although fairly extensive, the collection of pottery with painted figures and ornaments – commonly known as vases – cannot give even a general idea of the development and different schools of Greek ceramics. It was assembled in Rome, and therefore contains only those groups of Greek vases that were imported into central Italy regularly and in large numbers during the 6th and 5th centuries B. C., the time when Greek art and craftsmanship in general was at its height, and the Italian market was completely dominated by Greek ceramics. The pottery produced by the natives of Italy themselves, particularly the Etruscans, who were the most prominent, was of a cruder kind. The Etruscans occasionally tried to imitate the Greek vases. Such imitations are to be seen in Cabinet 1 (No. 47), and on top of Cabinet 2 (No. 151). Not until the political decline of Greece, from about 400 B. C. onwards, brought about an appreciable falling off of trade and industry did the Greek import trade dwindle. Painted vases were widely used in Italy for another hundred years; but they were now produced in the country itself, in Etruria, Campania, and the large Greek colonies in the south of Italy.

The vases displayed were all or nearly all found in graves in Etruria and the neighbouring districts; as was the common ancient usage, they had been buried with the dead in order that they might be used in the next world. Although found and used in Etruria, they are pure Greek in appearance and type: the different forms (drinking-bowls, pitchers, wine-jars, ointment-jars, etc.) correspond to the domestic habits of the Greeks, and the pictures show scenes from Greek legends, and from Greek daily life.

In the 6th-5th centuries B. C. the largest export to Etruria came from Athens; as a natural result, Attic vases form the larger part of the collection of Greek vases. Less strongly represented are Athens' competitors in the 6th century, Corinth (Nos. 1-8, 160-161), and Chalcis (Nos. 70 and 80).

Cabinet 1, left.

Top shelf, above: Corinthian vases and Italic imitations of these of 7th-6th centuries B. C., the earliest of the vase groups displayed, recognizable by the pale yellowish clay and the brownish-black "glaze". Real or fabulous animals form the main decorative motif (No. 7, ointment-jar with a picture of a siren, i. e. a human-headed bird), on large vessels often as a frieze (No. 1, a deep drinking-bowl: animal frieze showing a panther, a sphinx and a griffin). *Top shelf, below, and middle shelf:* Attic vases of the 6th century B. C., with black figures on a yellowish-red ground. The skin of the women is generally painted white. Of the pictures, the following may be singled out: No. 27, Silenus with a drinking-horn, stooping under the weight of a large wine-bowl. No. 10, Dionysus, crowned with ivy, and holding a large drinking-cup and trails of grape-vine. Some of the exploits of Hercules: No. 44, the struggle with Apollo for the Delphic tripod; No. 41, the battle with Triton; No. 40, the battle with the Nemean lion; No. 38 (by *"the Antimenes painter"*), Hercules brings the Erymanthian boar to Eurystheus; No. 42, the battle with the Amazons; No. 39, Hercules subdues the Cretan bull. – *Bottom shelf:* Vessel of dark clay with a faintly gleaming black surface ("bucchero"), a peculiar form of pottery which flourished particularly in Etruria in the 7th-6th centuries B. C.

Cabinet 1, right.

Top and middle shelves: Mainly Attic vases (No. 47 is an Etruscan imitation) of the 6th century B. C., with black figures on a yellowish-red ground. The pictures are for the most part roughly drawn. Many of them represent bacchic scenes, e. g. Nos. 16, 26, 29, 31, and 34. Theseus' battle with the Minotaur is shown on the amphora No. 47 and the drinking-bowl No. 48. – *Bottom shelf:* pottery of different periods, mostly Italic work. Two (281 and 282) are from the 7th-6th century B. C.

Cabinet 2, left and right.

Top and middle shelves: Attic vases of the 6th century B. C., with black figures on a yellowish-red ground. Among the most important are three water-jars (hydriai) showing a mythical bridal procession (No. 74), a quadriga seen from the front (No. 54, by *"the Antimenes painter"*), and a war-chariot in action (No. 56, belonging to the so-called *"Leagros group"*); the charioteer can be recognized by his long white robe. No. 52, a well-preserved amphora with an often-depicted, rather roughly executed picture: two heroes fighting, on the right and left a woman watching. – *Bottom shelf:* completely black "glazed" pottery vessels of the 4th-2nd centuries B. C., made in various Italic workshops, mainly in Etruria and Campania. Many imitate metal vessels in shape.

Cabinet 3.

Top and middle shelves: Vases from the finest period of Attic ceramics, about 530-400 B. C., with red figures on a dark ground (cf. Cabinet 4, top and middle shelves). The chief stages in the development of the style are represented, from strictly archaic art with its highly conventionalized rendering of the human figure, to the free style during and after the middle of the 5th century B. C. The favourite subjects of vase paintings now include pictures from daily life, especially the physical exercises of young Greeks (see drinking-bowl No. 107, made by "*the Foundry painter*", as was No. 111 in Cabinet 4), and their association with young women (bowl No. 114, attributed to "*the Penthesilea painter*"). – *Bottom shelf:* Vases of the 4th-3rd centuries B. C., with red figures on a dark ground, mostly Italic work, from factories in Etruria, Campania, Apulia, and Lucania.

Cabinet 4.

Top and middle shelves: Vases from the finest period of Attic ceramics, about 530-400 B. C., with red figures on a dark ground (as in Cabinet 3, top and middle shelves). These also depict physical exercises (drinking-bowls No. 111, by "*the Foundry painter*" (cf. No. 107, Cabinet 3), and No. 112, by "*the Brygos painter*") feasts and carousals (amphora No. 117 and bowl No. 115; a number of vases are known as "*the Thorvaldsen group*" after this bowl). Mythical and heroic subjects also occur: Ajax and Achilles at the chequer-board (drinking-bowl No. 100, made by *Oltos*), the fate of Actæon (amphora No. 99, by "*the Geras painter*"). In addition to Nos. 100 and 111-12, the most important vases from an artistic point of view include two fragments of large craters, No. 96, by "*the Altamura painter*", with a picture of Poseidon and a goddess, and No. 97, which like No. 101 belongs to the circle of the vase-painter *Polygnotos,* with a picture of Dionysus and Dithyrambus. – *Bottom shelf:* Vases of the 4th-3rd centuries B. C., with red figures on a dark ground (cf. Cabinet 3, bottom shelf).

BASEMENT

THORVALDSEN'S EARLY WORK,
HIS COLLECTIONS OF CASTS, PAINTINGS,
AND WATER-COLOURS, ETC.

THORVALDSEN'S EARLY WORK.
ROOM XLIII
at the foot of the stairs

654 STATUETTE. Bacchus and Ariadne. Original model,
Rome 1798.

657 —Achilles and Penthesilea. Original model, Rome
1801. Bequest by J.M.Thiele 1875.

661 BUST. Count A.P.Bernstorff, prime minister. Copenhagen 1795. Old cast. Presented by the Ministry of
Home Affairs 1922.

662 —Count A.P.Bernstorff. Original model. A modifi-
cation of No. 661 carried out in Rome, 1797.

673 RELIEF. Decoration above a gateway. Carved in wood
by Thorvaldsen in Copenhagen 1792 from a drawing by the naval sculptor F.C.Willerup, for No. 17,
Ny Vestergade. Presented by Den sjællandske Bon-
destands Sparekasse 1936.

674 —The Royal coat of arms, from the Court pharmacy,
25, Store Kongensgade. Painted sandstone. Copenhagen 1789. Presented by Mr. Ibsen, Court pharma-
cist, 1882.

689 PORTRAIT MEDALLION. E.H.Løffler, drawing-master at the Academy of Fine Arts. Original model,
Copenhagen 1796. Presented by Professor E. Utzon-Frank 1926.

ROOM XLIV

672 RELIEF. Cupid resting. Original model, Copenhagen
     1789. Awarded the large silver medal of the Acad-
     emy of Fine Arts. Presented by the Academy 1855.

675 —Heliodorus driven out of the temple. Original
     model, Copenhagen 1791. Awarded the small gold
     medal of the Academy of Fine Arts. Presented by
     the Academy 1918.

676 —Achilles and Priam. Original model, Copenhagen
     1791. Presented by the Academy of Fine Arts 1887.

683 —The Seasons. Original model, Copenhagen 1794.
     Made for Prince Frederik's (later Christian X's)
     palace at Amalienborg, from N. Abildgaard's com-
     position. Lent by the Royal Gallery of Fine Arts
     1925.

684 —The Hours. Original model, Copenhagen 1794.
     Made for Prince Frederik's (later Christian X's)
     palace at Amalienborg from N. Abildgaard's com-
     position. Lent by the Royal Gallery of Fine Arts
     1925.

ROOM XLV

651 STATUETTE. Mother and two children. Original
     model, Copenhagen, about 1793. Purchased at the
     sale of the effects of the painter N. Abildgaard's
     widow in 1850.

652 —The Muse Euterpe. Original model, painted plaster.
     Copenhagen 1794. Sketch model for a statue in Prince
     Frederik's (later Christian X's) palace at Amalien-
     borg, from a composition by N. Abildgaard. Present-
     ed by the Academy of Fine Arts 1855.

653 —The Muse Terpsichore. Original model, painted

plaster. Copenhagen 1794. Sketch model for a statue in Prince Frederik's (later Christian X's) palace at Amalienborg, from a composition by N. Abildgaard. Presented by the Academy of Fine Arts 1855.

656 STATUETTE. Venus and Cupid. Original model, about 1800.

677 RELIEF. Hercules and Omphale. Copenhagen 1792. Cast.

678 —The apostles Peter and John healing a lame man before the gate of the temple. Original model, Copenhagen 1793. Awarded the large gold medal of the Academy of Fine Arts. Presented by the Academy 1918.

682 —King Numa Pompilius conversing with the nymph Egeria in her grotto. Copenhagen 1794. Cast.

679 PORTRAIT MEDALLION. Louise Augusta, Duchess of Augustenborg. Original model, painted and gilded plaster. Copenhagen 1793. Purchased 1911.

680 —The actor Michael Rosing. Copenhagen 1793. Painted plaster. Purchased 1910.

681 —The actress Johanne Cathrine Rosing, née Olsen, wife of the above. Copenhagen 1793. Painted plaster. Purchased 1910.

685 —Simon Jensen, book-keeper and administrator of the Danish West Indian Trading Company. Original model, Copenhagen 1793.

686 —Eleonora Maria Jensen, née Weygaard, wife of the above. Original model, Copenhagen 1793.

687 —Simon Jensen's children, on the left Anna Birgitte Margrethe, later Glahn by marriage. Original model, Copenhagen 1793. 685-87 were presented in 1856 by C.J.Glahn.

688   PORTRAIT MEDALLION. Count A. P. Bernstorff. Original model, painted and gilded plaster. Copenhagen 1796. Purchased 1911.

690   —Konferensraad P.J.Monrad. Painted plaster. Copenhagen. Probably a cast.

691   —Cecilia Kirstine Monrad, née Martin, wife of the above. Painted plaster. Copenhagen. Probably a cast.

692   —Probably Konferensraad Bernt Anker. Terracotta. Original model, Copenhagen. Purchased 1879 from the effects of C.F.Wilckens.

A896   Konferensraad Holger Christian Reiersen. Original model (?). Bronzed plaster. Copenhagen 1793. Purchased 1953.

A897   Charlotte Kirstine Reiersen, née Studsgaard, wife of the above. Original model (?). Bronzed plaster. Copenhagen 1793. Purchased 1953.

ROOM XLVI

655   STATUE. Pollux. Copy, approximately 1/3 size, of one of the ancient horse-tamers on Monte Cavallo, Rome. Original model, 1799.

663   BUST. The philosopher Tyge Rothe. Copenhagen 1796. Marble (Thorvaldsen, Rome 1797). Probably Thorvaldsen's first marble work.

664   —Madam Høyer, the mother of the painter Christian Fædder Høyer. 1809. Marble (Thorvaldsen). Bequest by the painter C.F.Høyer 1855.

665   —Raphael. Marble (Thorvaldsen, 1800). Copy of the bust of Raphael by Pietro Paolo Naldini, placed in the Pantheon, Rome, in 1674, and moved to "La Protomoteca" on the Capitol in 1820.

666 BUST. Agrippa. Marble (Thorvaldsen, 1799-1800).
     Copy of an antique bust.

667 —Cicero. Marble (Thorvaldsen, 1799-1800). Copy
     of an antique bust.

668 —Cicero. Marble (Thorvaldsen, 1799-1800). Copy of
     an antique bust.

669 —Homer. Marble (Thorvaldsen, 1799). Copy of an
     antique bust.

Nos. 665 and 669 were bought at the sale of the effects of
the painter N.Abildgaard's widow in 1850; Nos. 666-68
were presented by the Academy of Fine Arts in 1855.

ROOM XLVII-XLVIII

Display of plaster casts of Thorvaldsen's works, from the
Museum's plaster workshop. See separate sales catalogue.

THORVALDSEN'S COLLECTION OF CASTS

*Corridors A and B, Rooms XLIX, LX, and LXI, and part of the storage
corridor contain Thorvaldsen's collection of casts of works by other artists;
most of these are antique, but there are a few pieces of later date. The collection gives an impression of the works that formed the basis of the view
of art held by Thorvaldsen and his contemporaries.*

CORRIDOR A

I. ANTIQUE STATUES AND STATUETTES

6-7 Two statuettes of women from the temple of Aphaia
     on Aegina. – The two figures, which originally flanked
     the large palmette acroterium on the west pediment
     of the temple, were excavated in 1811 together with
     many other fragments of sculpture. The whole of
     this find was acquired by King Ludwig of Bavaria
     (at that time Crown Prince), who entrusted the res-

toration of the pediment groups to Thorvaldsen (1816-17). The statuettes, with their archaic appearance and treatment of the drapery possibly formed the models for his statue "Hope" (Room VIII). The sculpture of the Aphaia temple, now in the Glyptothek in Munich, is from about 490-80 B. C.

8   Head of a helmeted warrior from the Aphaia temple on Aegina. From the east pediment, which showed the Aeginetans fighting the Trojans.

26 From the Parthenon on the Acropolis at Athens. The upper part of a group of three seated women.

27 Head of a horse, from the Parthenon on the Acropolis at Athens.

28 Torso of a reclining man, commonly called Ilissus. From the Parthenon on the Acropolis at Athens.

29 The so-called Weber-Laborde head. Nose, mouth, and chin restored by the Venetian sculptor *Ferrari*. The original (now in Paris) was in Thorvaldsen's day in Venice.

Nos. 26 and 27, and probably No. 29, come from the east pediment of the Parthenon, which showed the birth of Athene. No. 28 is from the west pediment of the temple, which showed the battle of Athene and Poseidon for Attica. The Parthenon pediments were completed about 432 B. C. The originals were acquired by Lord Elgin in 1801-03, and were placed in the British Museum in 1816.

31 Apollo; the so-called Apollino, Florence.

32 Venus de Medici, Florence.

33 The Capitoline Venus, Museo Capitolino, Rome.

Nos. 32 and 33 derive from works of the late 4th century B. C. Both show the goddess of love rising from the sea or from her bath.

34 Small kneeling Venus in her bath. By the Hellenistic sculptor *Doidalsas.*

35 Cupid bending his bow. Ascribed to *Lysippus,* the last great sculptor of the 4th century B. C.

36 Two children kissing each other (Cupid and Psyche). Museo Capitolino, Rome. Group of the Hellenistic period.

37 The so-called Psyche of Capua, possibly a fragment of an Aphrodite statue. Naples.

39 Standing man. Pasticcio (i. e. a statue put together by a modern restorer using random fragments of different antique sculptures. Such pasticci were fairly frequently made in the studios of Italian sculptors of the baroque period and later). The head is a replica of the Belvedere Hermes (No. 38, Corridor B). The torso however belongs to a statue of the 5th century B. C., the so-called Diadumenos of *Polycleitus.* The Glyptothek, Munich.

41 Standing Muse. The Glyptothek, Munich. Of the Hellenistic period; restored by Thorvaldsen, as Clio, carrying a scroll and style.

42 Seated Muse. The Vatican, Rome. Of the Hellenistic period.

43 Upper part of a female figure wearing a wreath of flowers. Found in Hadrian's villa, now in the Museo Capitolino, Rome.

46 Head and shoulders of the so-called Westmacott ephebe in the British Museum, London. Roman copy after *Polycleitus.*

48 Discus thrower. Found in 1792 by the Via Appia, Rome, and now in the Vatican. Ascribed to the sculptor *Naucydes* (first half of the 4th century B. C.).The head is antique, but belongs to another statue.

49   Boy removing a thorn. Bronze statue in the Palazzo dei Conservatori, Rome. Roman work in Greek style.

50   Small girl playing dice. Berlin. Hellenistic figure.

52   Seated boy with bunches of grapes. National Museum, Copenhagen, formerly in the possession of Capece Latro, Archbishop of Tarento, and of Christian VIII.

53   Boy eating grapes.

56   Torso of a boy, possibly Ganymede. Berlin. 4th century B. C.

57   Torso of a man. Villa Albani, Rome. Roman copy of a torso of the first half of the 5th century B. C.; the long curls on the shoulder indicate an Apollo statue.

58   Torso of a youth. Berlin.

59   Torso of a running boy.

60   Torso of a Praxitelean female figure. The Glyptothek, Munich. Restored by Thorvaldsen.

61   Small torso of a female figure, found in the ruins of Carthaea on the island of Ceos by the Danish archaeologist P. O. Brøndsted.

62   Torso of a woman. Schloss Tegel, near Berlin.

93   Head of a horse. Florence.

94   Head of a horse. From the equestrian statue of Nonius Balbus the Younger, Naples.

95   Eagle with spread wings.

2. ANTIQUE BUSTS AND HEADS

99   The Otricoli Jupiter. The Vatican.

100   Poseidon. The Vatican. Hellenistic.

102   Head of the so-called Velletri Pallas Athene. Now in the Louvre, Paris.

104   Head of Apollo Belvedere (cf. No. 30, Room XLIX).

105   Apollo. British Museum, London.

106   Venus.

107   Venus. Found in the thermae of Diocletian in Rome,
        1805; now in the Vatican.

109   Apollo. Museo Capitolino, Rome.

110   Herm of Zeus Ammon. The Vatican.

111   Bearded head of Bacchus.

112   Herm of a bearded Dionysus.

113   Head of Dionysus. Museo Capitolino, Rome. 4th
        century B. C.

114-116   Satyrs. Nos. 114-115, Munich.

117   Head of a statue of Pan. British Museum, London.

118   Bacchante.

119   Bearded river-god or rustic god; mask.

120   Mask of a so-called head of Zeus. Villa Albani, Rome.

121   Rome; identifiable by reliefs of she-wolves on either
        side of the helmet. Formerly in the Villa Borghese,
        now in the Louvre.

123-124   Colossal heads. From the so-called horse-tamers
        (the Dioscuri) now placed on Monte Cavallo, Rome.
        From the time of Hadrian.

127   Paris in a Phrygian cap.

128-129   Heads from the Laocoon group in the Vatican.
        No. 128, Laocoon himself, No. 129, head of one of
        his sons looking up at his father in terror.

130-133   Heads from the large Niobe group in Florence.
        No. 130, Niobe, No. 131, one of Niobe's daughters,
        Nos. 132-133, two of her sons. The group is prob-
        ably the work of *Scopas* (middle of the 4th century
        B. C.).

134   Hero. Margam Park, England.

135   Hero. Formerly held to be Alexander, but more prob-
        ably a dying hero in Pergamenian style. Florence.

136   Mask of an Amazon head, possibly of the "Amazone
        Mattei" in the Vatican.

137-138   Blind Homer. Ideal heads. Both from a bust in
          Naples, No. 137 with certain minor changes.

142   The Cynic Antisthenes. Possibly a cast of a bust in
          Naples.

143   The philosopher Theophrastus. Mask of a herm in
          the Villa Albani, Rome.

144   The Stoic and scientist Poseidonius. Naples.

146   The orator Demosthenes.

147   Mask, formerly held to be Hannibal. Villa Albani,
          Rome.

149   Mask with Attic helmet, formerly held to be Mil-
          tiades. The Louvre, Paris.

150   Alexander the Great; head of the so-called Alexander
          Rondanini statue in the Glyptothek, Munich, restored
          by Thorvaldsen.

157   Head of a priest. The Vatican.

175   The Stoic Chrysippus. Museo Capitolino, Rome.

176   An elderly man, a so-called portrait of Seneca.

177   Unknown man.

178   Unknown man; a Roman of the Antonine period.
          Villa Albani, Rome.

179   Unknown man.

180   Hellenistic (?) warrior. Naples.

182   Diomedes; head of a statue in the Glyptothek, Mu-
          nich. Probably derives from an original by *Cresilas*.

185   The comedy writer Menander.

194   Hellenistic prince (Antiochus III of Syria?). The
          Louvre, Paris.

195   Helmeted man. Villa Albani, Rome.

199   Ideal head of a woman.

200   Female portrait herm. The Vatican.

203   An African athlete; head of a black marble statue in
          Vienna.

3. ANTIQUE RELIEFS

266 Fragment showing a horseman. Once the property of the painter Camuccini, now in the Vatican. Boeotian tombstone of the period of the Parthenon sculptures, and influenced by them.

267 Fragment. Gaea entrusts the infant Erichthonius to Athene; at the side one foot of Hephaestus can be seen. The Vatican.

268 Greek tombstone (stele) of a young man, shown reading a scroll. In Grottaferrata near Rome. Beginning of the 4th century B. C.

270-271 Dancers. The Vatican. Neo-Attic style.

272-273 Dancers. The Uffizi Galleries, Florence. Neo-Attic style.

274 Woman with a sacrificial bull. Neo-Attic relief, the motif of which derives from the balustrade of the Nike temple, Athens.

277 Two veiled women, one seated on a rock, the other standing. The Vatican.

279 From a sepulchral relief: a youth and a sorrowing woman parting. The Vatican.

280 Greek votive relief. Dedicated (by the small figure of a man on the left) to two deities, a seated man, who probably held a sceptre, and a standing woman, whom Thorvaldsen may have had in mind when he made his statue of Hebe (Room VI, No. 38). The Vatican. End of the 5th - beginning of the 4th century B. C.

281 Youth between hetaerae. Naples. Roman copy of a Hellenistic original.

304 Rustic idyll. The Vatican. First century.

306 Cupid driving two wild boars; at the side an altar.
The Vatican.

341 Wedding scene.

342 Man and woman with a bull-calf and game.
341 and 342 are casts of Roman terracotta, so-called
Campana, reliefs.

345 Satyr and maenad. Villa Albani, Rome. Campana relief.

4. WORKS OF A LATER DATE

3* *Andrea del Verrocchio:* Half-length portrait of Cosimo
de Medici. Relief. In marble in Berlin.

6* *Giovanni da Bologna:* The Journey to Calvary. Relief.
In bronze in the Church of SS Annunziata, Florence.

7* Basin decorated with an outer circle of tritons, nereids,
and sea-monsters, an inner circle of four river-gods,
and in the centre a medallion containing the portrait
of Charles I, Duke of Mantua. Italy, 17th century.

10* *François Duquesnoy* (?): Hovering putto. 17th century.

11* Hovering putto. 17th century.

CORRIDOR B

I. ANTIQUE STATUES

5 She-wolf, the symbol of Rome. In bronze in the
Palazzo dei Conservatori, Rome. Here without the
sucking twins of the original, which are not contemporary with the animal, but derive from a restoration at the time of the Renaissance.

38 The Belvedere Hermes. The Vatican. The original
has been ascribed to *Praxiteles*.

40 Silenus, holding the infant Bacchus. The Louvre,
Paris. The original is probably of the school of
Lysippus.

45   The child Ganymede, seized by the eagle. The Vatican.

47   The Borghese warrior. Now in the Louvre, Paris.
     Hellenistic work.

51   Seated boy with a duck.

55   The Belvedere torso; possibly that of a seated Silenus.
     The Vatican. Hellenistic work.

2. ANTIQUE BUSTS AND HEADS

152   So-called L. Junius Brutus, first consul of Rome. In
      bronze in the Palazzo dei Conservatori, Rome.

153   So-called Brutus minor, the murderer of Caesar.
      Museo Capitolino, Rome.

154   The emperor Augustus as a young man. The Vatican.

155   The emperor Augustus. From Velletri; now added to
      a toga-clad statue in the Louvre.

156   The emperor Augustus. In bronze in the Vatican library.

159   Mask of a Roman (formerly held to be Galba). The
      Louvre.

160   The emperor Trajan. The Louvre.

161   The emperor Trajan. The original has been lost.

162   Ælius Verus. The Louvre.

167   The emperor Antoninus Pius; the back of the head is
      missing. From a version of the portrait in the Sala
      a Croce Greca in the Vatican.

168   The emperor Marcus Aurelius as a young man. Museo
      Capitolino, Rome.

169   The emperor Marcus Aurelius when older.

171   The emperor Marcus Aurelius. Colossal head, from
      the equestrian statue on the Capitol, Rome.

172   The emperor Lucius Verus; mask.

174   The emperor Caracalla. Naples.

181   Young man with curled hair and side-whiskers.

183-184, 188-192 Portraits of elderly clean-shaven Romans. No. 184 is in Naples, No. 189 in Florence.

196 Unidentified woman, portrayed as a statue of the so-called Pudicitia type.

197 Unidentified woman, of the Claudian period.

198 The empress Sabina, wife of Hadrian. Museo Capitolino, Rome.

3. ANTIQUE RELIEFS

294 Vase with dancing maenads. Villa Albani, Rome.

295 Vase with dancing satyrs and corybantes. The Vatican.

297 Jupiter, Minerva, and Apollo. Roman.

298 Well-head, (puteal), showing the legends of Hylas and Narcissus. For the Hylas legend, cf. Thorvaldsen's relief with the same motif, No. 484, Room XIV.

ROOM XLIX

ANTIQUE STATUE

30 The Apollo Belvedere, famous since the time of the Renaissance, held to be a Roman copy of a work by *Leochares* of the second half of the 4th century B. C. The Vatican. The statue is supposed to have been of importance for Thorvaldsen's statue of Jason.

ANTIQUE BUSTS

165 Antinous, the favourite of the emperor Hadrian, as Bacchus. The Vatican.

170 The emperor Marcus Aurelius. Colossal head, apparently deriving from the equestrian statue on the Capitol in Rome.

ROOM L

180   STATUE. *Thorvaldsen.* Dancing girl. 1837. Marble.

PAINTINGS

103   *Abraham Teerlink.* Italian landscape.

221   *H. Harder.* Landscape near Sorø.

222   *Julius Hellesen.* Danish landscape. 1843.

229   *Johannes Jensen.* Old sailor. 1843.

240   *F. C. Kiærskou.* Landscape in the Bavarian Tyrol. 1846.

250   *G. E. Libert.* Moors near Aalborg. 1839.

257   *Thomas Læssøe.* Valløby Church. 1839.

260   *H. D. C. Martens.* St Peter's, from the *Via Sacra,* north of Rome.

261   —The Capitol, from the colonnade of the Palazzo dei Conservatori. Rome.

264   *Anton Melbye.* Dutch koff and ship of the line in a moderate breeze.

289   *C. Schleisner.* Genre piece. 1838.

294   *F. Thøming.* American brig at anchor in the Bay of Naples. 1827.

ROOM LI

PAINTINGS

70   *F. Diofebi.* The side steps from the Capitol to the church of S. Maria in Aracoeli. Rome. 1825.

71   —The ruined temple of Mars Ultor. Rome. 1826.

81   *Beniamino de Francesco.* Italian landscape with mythological figures (Æneas and the Sibyl). 1838.

83   *E. Landesio.* Italian landscape. 1838.

99   *Joseph Severn.* Italian woman and her daughter. 1831.

124   *Leo von Klenze.* The harbour at Pirano. Istria.

133 A *F. Nerly*. Italian landscape.

174   *J. N. Glowacki*. Tyrolean landscape. 1835.

175   *Orest Kiprenski*. Armenian priest.

275   *J. Mohr*. Bavarian landscape. 1840.

ROOM LII

RELIEF, by the window. *H. E. Freund:* The moon-goddess
Selene. Plaster models for a pilaster capital on the main
facade of the Museum, executed in sandstone by *Johann
Scholl* in 1843.

PAINTINGS

86 A *M. Pacetti*. View of the Tiber, showing St Peter's and
      the Castle of St. Angelo. Rome. 1835.

106   *Heinrich Bürkel*. Scene in front of an Italian osteria.
      1831.

107   —The performing bears come to an Italian village.
      1831.

114   *F. Elsasser*. View from the ancient theatre in Taormina.
      1838.

116   *Philipp von Foltz*. Sleeping Italian beggar girl. 1836.

117   —Composition sketch illustrating Uhland's poem
      "Des Sängers Fluch". 1837.

136 A *F. Overbeck*. The Good Shepherd. Lent by the Ny
      Carlsberg Glyptotek, 1943.

142   *J. C. Reinhart*. Scene from the Roman Campagna. 1823.

152   *J. Riepenhausen*. Venus and Adonis.

158   *G. Schick*. Landscape with biblical figures (Ruth and
      Boaz). The landscape in the middle distance and
      background is the work of *J. A. Koch*.

159   *J. H. Schilbach*. The Forum Romanum. 1825.

302 A *H. Reinhold*. Scene from the Isle of Capri. Unfinished.

ROOM LIII

4 STATUETTE. *Pietro Galli.* The invention of the syrinx.
Pan with the pipe, and Cupid. Marble.

PAINTINGS

82 A *Vincenzo Giovannini.* A chemist in his laboratory.

85 *F. Storelli.* Italian landscape. 1833.

90 *T. Gudin.* The coast near Naples. 1837.

97 *G. Lazzerini.* Copy after *F. M. Granet:* The choir of
the capuchin monastery near the Piazza Barberini,
Rome.

118 *C. W. von Heideck.* Scene from the defence of a Spanish
town during a guerilla war. 1841.

153 *J. Riepenhausen.* Cupid instructing two young girls.

154 —Bramante presenting Raphael to Pope Julius II.

155 —A second-hand bookseller in a Roman street.

167 *M. Wittmer.* Æsop seated on a plinth above a spring,
telling his fables to the people. 1841.

169 *Karl Markó.* Lake Nemi. 1834.

252 *J. L. Lund.* Italian landscape.

ROOM LIV

RELIEFS, by the window. *H. E. Freund:* The moon-goddess
Selene and Helios the sun-god. Plaster models for pilaster
capitals on the main facade of the Museum, executed in
sandstone by *Johann Scholl* in 1843.

PAINTINGS

7 *Italian artist* of the 16th century. The Virgin with her
family.

8 *Italian artist* of the 16th century. Portrait of a man.

9   *Sofonisba Anguisciola.* Portrait of a young woman. About 1550.

12   A halt during the Flight into Egypt. Copy of a painting in the Galleria Nazionale, Parma, ascribed to *Ippolito Scarsella (Scarsellino).*

14   Virgin and Child. Copy of a variation on *Lelio Orsi*'s Madonna della Ghiara in Tempio della Beata Vergine della Ghiara, Reggio Emilia.

15   Venus and Cupid. Copy of a painting by *G. B. Paggi* in the Palazzo Bianco, Genoa.

25   The Descent of the Holy Ghost. Copy of a painting by *Jacopo Bassano* in the Museo Civico, Bassano.

31   *Crescenzio Onofri.* Landscape.

32   —Landscape.

33   *A. Locatelli.* Landscape.

44A   *P. Brill.* Mountain landscape.

45   *In the manner of Pieter Brueghel the Younger.* The temptations of St Anthony.

47   *Dutch artist of the 17th century.* Man with a wine-glass.

48   *Lieve Verschuir.* Seascape.

49   *J. F. van Bloemen.* Landscape.

51   *In the manner of A. F. Boudewyns and Peeter Bout.* A ferry.

52   —Road beside a river.

53   —Crowd scene.

56   *Hendrik Voogd.* Italian landscape.

306   *Italian artist* of the 17th century. The ecstasy of St Francis. Miniature.

DRAWINGS

(On the window wall).

Thorvaldsen. Self-portrait. About 1786.

Unknown artist. Portrait of Thorvaldsen. About 1797.

ROOM LV

On the window wall: *Jørgen Sonne's frieze* on the facades of the Museum; lithographic reproduction by *F.C.Lund*, coloured by the painter *Mimi Bille* c. 1891-92 (continued in Room LVI).

COPIES OF ITALIAN AND DUTCH PAINTINGS

34 Madonna and Child. *Ditlev Blunck*, after *Perugino*.
35 "Madonna del Granduca". *Ditlev Blunck*, after *Raphael*.
37 "The violin player". *C.Eggers*, after *Sebastian del Piombo*.
40 The education of Cupid. Old copy after *Titian*.
54 Portrait of a man. *Ditlev Blunck*, after *B. van der Helst*.

ROOM LVI

On the window wall: *Jørgen Sonne's frieze* on the facades of the Museum; lithographic reproduction by *F.C.Lund*, coloured by the painter *Mimi Bille* c. 1891-92 (continued from Room LV).

DRAWINGS AND WATER-COLOURS

2 *Antonio Aquaroni*. The Arch of Titus, Rome. 1825. Pencil and sepia.
3 —The colonnade, St Peter's Square. Pencil and sepia.
6 *Thorvaldsen*. Self-portrait. Rome, September 8th, 1811. Pencil and black and white crayon. Purchased 1865.
12 *F.Diofebi*. Interior, from the Lateran Church, Rome. Water-colour.
15 *J.Ferrari*. Pope Leo XII being carried in procession

through the colonnade of St Peter's Square. Pencil and sepia.

161 *L. Dupré.* Young Greek. Water-colour.

168 *George Augustus Wallis.* Historical landscape, with sacrificial procession. The figures are undoubtedly the work of *Thorvaldsen.* Pencil and sepia.

172 —Historical landscape. "Ave Maria". The figures are undoubtedly the work of *Thorvaldsen.* Sepia and water-colour.

173 *W. Wyld.* Algiers harbour. 1833. Water-colour.

199 *C. H. Kniep.* View of Naples. 1819. Pencil.

202 *J. A. Koch.* Dante and Virgil are carried to Malebolge, the Eighth Circle of Hell, on the back of the monster Geryon. Composition by *Thorvaldsen.* Water-colour.

263 —Boaz and Ruth. Water-colour.

265 —Lautenbrunnertal, Switzerland. Water-colour.

282 *Rudolf Meyer.* Waterfall near Tivoli. Water-colour.

284 *Wilhelm Noack.* Drawing after a painting by *L. Robert:* The interior of the church of S. Paolo fuori le mura on the day after the fire, 1823. Ink and sepia.

286 *J. C. Reinhart.* Heroic landscape. 1813. Sepia.

289A —Landscape with a waterfall. Water-colour. Lent by the Ny Carlsberg Glyptotek, 1943.

297 *J. H. Schilbach.* Tyrolean landscape. Water-colour.

301 *J. Steingrübel.* View of Pescia. 1834. Water-colour.

303 *C. Werner.* The hall of the Council of Ten in the Doge's Palace, Venice. 1833. Water-colour.

315 *J. C. Dahl.* Landscape near Civita Castellana. 1817. Ink.

325A *Ditlev Blunck.* Thorvaldsen and his fellow voyagers in 1838 on board the frigate "Rota", during his journey home. 1838. Pencil. Purchased 1882.

No. 325 A. Blunck: Thorvaldsen and his fellow voyagers on board the frigate "Rota" during his journey home.

1 Thorvaldsen. 2 Captain Dahlerup. 3 and 4 Lieutenant Commanders Fisker and Liebman. 5, 6, and 7 Lieutenants M. Suenson, Flensborg and Thulstrup. 8, 9, 10, 11, 12, 13, and 14 Second Lieutenants C. A. Meyer, C. Wulff, Kinch, A. Wilde, Buchwald, Hedemann, and Jacobsen. 15 Blankensteiner, secretary. 16 Bisserup, purser. 17 Krieger, Chief Surgeon. 18 Hansen, Second Surgeon. 19 Brincken, Chief Officer. 20 H. J. Dahlerup, son of the Captain. 21 J. F. Frøhlich, composer and conductor. 22 D. Blunck, painter. 23 Wilhelm Matthiä, sculptor.

327 *Asmus Jacob Carstens.* The dance of the Muses on Helicon. Pencil.

330 —The giants attacking Olympus. Water-colour.

379 *C. F. F. Stanley.* Design for the main front of a theatre. 1803. Ink.

406 *Unidentified artist.* A billiard-room. Water-colour.

418 —The shore at Carrara: two large blocks of marble being hoisted on board a ship drawn up on the beach. Pencil, ink, and white paint.

420 *Unidentified artist.* Copy of the ancient mosaic floor in the Sala Rotunda of the Vatican. Watercolour.

ROOM LVII

WORKS BY THORVALDSEN

341A RELIEF. The dance of the Muses on Helicon. 1804. Marble (Thorvaldsen). Unfinished.

589A —Christmas joy in heaven. Nysø, 1842. Marble (Thorvaldsen). Unfinished.

503A —Four fragments of the marble version of the Alexander frieze, part of which was saved from the fire which destroyed Christiansborg Palace in 1884. Executed in Thorvaldsen's studio in Rome.

The *showcase* contains further fragments of the same frieze, presented by the Ministry of Home Affairs in 1919, together with the fragments mentioned above.

PORTRAITS OF THORVALDSEN

BUST. *Wilhelm Matthiä.* Thorvaldsen. 1833. Plaster.

—*Unknown artist,* possibly *George Rennie.* Thorvaldsen. Marble. Presented in 1921 by B.H.Jacobsen, Esq., London.

—*Pietro Bienaimé.* Thorvaldsen. 1826. Plaster. Presented in 1914 by Madame Vincenza Aubert de Rossi, Rome.

—*Pietro Tenerani.* Thorvaldsen. Cast of the marble version of 1824 in the Accademia di San Luca, Rome. Lent by the Ny Carlsberg Glyptotek, 1943.

ROOM LVIII

PORTRAITS OF THORVALDSEN AND
PERSONAL RELICS

The showcase under the window contains various objects and portraits connected with Thorvaldsen, among them two coloured portraits of Anders Grønlund, Attorney, and his wife, drawn by Thorvaldsen c. 1795, and a photograph of the daguerreotype of Thorvaldsen taken by *A.-C.-T. Neubourg* in 1840, a year after the invention of photography.

PAINTINGS, DRAWINGS ETC.

131 A *Dietrich Wilhelm Lindau.* Thorvaldsen. Oil-painting, c. 1825. Purchased 1888.

205   *Emil Bærentzen.* The actress Johanne Luise Heiberg. Oil-painting. 1841.

218 A *J. V. Gertner.* Thorvaldsen. Oil-painting, c. 1839. Presented by the Barony of Holstenshus in 1923.

220 B *Constantin Hansen.* Jonas Collin, titular Privy Councillor, Chairman of the Thorvaldsen's Museum Committee. Oil-painting. 1851. Presented in 1851 by a group of Collin's friends on the occasion of his fiftieth year in office.

262 A   *H. D. C. Martens.* Pope Leo XII visits Thorvaldsen's studios near the Piazza Barberini, Rome, on St Luke's Day (October 18th), 1826. Oil-painting. 1830. Lent by the Royal Museum of Fine Arts, 1920.

282 A *Paul Mila.* Thorvaldsen. 1823. Drawing. Pencil and black crayon. Purchased 1935.

312   *C. W. Balsgaard.* Copy of C. W. Eckersberg's portrait of Thorvaldsen executed in 1814. Overglaze painted on porcelain.

355A *Troels Lund*. Piazza Barberini with the Palazzo Barbe-
       rini, Rome. Water-colour. Purchased 1941.

*   *   *

The *cabinet* against the rear wall contains clothes and weapons which belonged to Thorvaldsen. These include two
smocks, caps worn by him in the studio and at home, his
uniforms, as a member of the French Academy in Rome
(with green embroidery) and of the Accademia di San Luca
(with the black silk cape), both with the tricorns and swords
belonging to them, his dresscoat and top hat (all presented
in 1875 by Captain J.C. Jacobsen of the Carlsberg Breweries);
also his stick and lantern, a pair of travelling pistols, and a
brown leather lotto bag from Nysø.

*   *   *

STATUETTE. *Wilhelm Matthiä*. Thorvaldsen. 1838.
         Plaster.
—*P. Ricco*. Thorvaldsen. Rome, 1834. Baked clay.
         Lent by the Ny Carlsberg Glyptotek, 1943.
—Possibly *Søren Seidelin Winther*. Thorvaldsen. Ivory.
         Bequest from Mrs. Stephanie Kehlet, née Møller,
         1925.
—*Unknown artist*. Thorvaldsen. Bronze. Purchased
         1933.
20A BUST. *C. D. Rauch*. Thorvaldsen. 1816. Plaster. Pre-
         sented by Herr Eichler, plasterer, Berlin. 1870.
6   PORTRAIT MEDALLION. *Unknown artist*. Thorvald-
         sen. Bronze. From a self-portrait drawn by Thor-
         valdsen (cf. No. 6, Room LVI).
7   —*Desiderio Cesari*. Thorvaldsen. 1825. Gilded bronze.
8   —*Desiderio Cesari*. Thorvaldsen. 1833. Gilded bronze.

8A —*Franz Woltreck*. Thorvaldsen. 1836. Bronze. Presented by Johan Hansen, Consul-General, 1940.

16B RELIEF. *P.F.Rauner*. Thorvaldsen. 1844. Wax. Purchased 1904. *Jørgen Sonne*. Thorvaldsen. About 1846. Coloured plaster. Trial section for the frieze on the facade of the Museum. Purchased 1938.

ROOM LIX

115   *F.Flor*. Elisa Paulsen, Thorvaldsen's daughter (wife of Colonel Fritz Paulsen). Oil-painting. 1838.

121A *Eduard Heuss*. Thorvaldsen. Oil-painting. 1834. Lent by the Ny Carlsberg Glyptotek, 1916.

132   *Eduard Magnus*. Thorvaldsen in his working clothes. Oil-painting c. 1825.

174A *Apollinari Goravski*. Thorvaldsen. Copy made in 1852 of the painting by *Orest Kiprenski* of 1833 in the Russian Museum, Leningrad. Presented in 1937 by Johan Hansen, Consul-General.

*   *   *

Below the window is a large *iron box*, made by a Copenhagen smith named Berg as his test piece for the rank of master craftsman; Thorvaldsen bought it after his return from Italy in 1842 to store his valuables in, but never used it. See C.F.Wilckens: "Træk af Thorvaldsen's Konstner- og Omgangsliv", Copenhagen 1874, p. 82.

*   *   *

The cabinet against the rear wall contains a number of *death masks,* some of famous persons, some unidentified, used by Thorvaldsen to some extent when making portrait busts. There are also a few *life masks*. Above, Thorvaldsen's death mask, crowned with laurel, and a life mask, made by Count *Savarelli,* probably c. 1810. Below, death masks of Napoleon, Charles XII of Sweden (recent investigations have cast some doubt on this identification), the popes Pius VII and Leo XII, Cardinal Consalvi, General Schwarzenberg, the Duke of Leuchtenberg, August von Goethe (son of the poet), Baron A. E. von Eichthal, the painter Heinrich Reinhold, Georg Zoëga, Jacob Baden, M. G. Bindesbøll (received in 1892 from the estate of the sculptor F. G. Hertzog, as a gift from his sister, Mrs. C. B. Jensen), and Madam Høyer (mother of the painter C. Fædder Høyer). In the middle of the cabinet are the life mask of Goethe (executed in 1807 by *Karl Gottlob Weisser),* and a portrait head of Sir Thomas Maitland, possibly by the sculptor *Paolo Prossalenti.*

ROOM LX

CASTS OF ANTIQUE SCULPTURE

By the window are fragments of statues (hands, arms, feet, etc.) presumably used as study material in Thorvaldsen's studio. In addition the following may be mentioned:

257   Apollonian votive relief. Apollo with his lyre, accompanied by his mother and sister, before the goddess of Victory. The original is in the Villa Albani.

260-265   Jupiter, Juno, Mercury, Minerva, Mars, and Venus. Six reliefs from the bases of incense altars, which now form the lower part of the Barberini candelabra in the Vatican. Neo-Attic. Found in Hadrian's villa in the 17th century.

285   A horse-racing genius. Fragment of a relief.

292-293   Two sides of a low, quadrangular marble altar, probably the base of a censer (thymiaterion), with winged chimeras at the corners.

292   Bacchus brings joy to mankind. The bearded Bacchus and his train are shown entering a dwelling where a man and his wife are reclining at table; a child satyr removes the god's sandals, while another supports him.

293   The purification of the soul, represented by a butterfly (Psyche), which two weeping cupids are burning in two torches over an incense altar. On either side are two centaurs with Bacchic attributes; one is carrying a youthful zither-playing satyr on his back, the other is kneeling on one knee and putting up his hand to help the bacchante on his back to dismount. Relief from the Villa Negroni, in the Vatican.

299   The giants warring against the gods. Relief from the front of a Roman sarcophagus in the Vatican.

302-303   The Seasons, personified as reclining female figures with little genii. Relief from the front of a Roman sarcophagus in the Vatican; it has erroneously been placed on the so-called Hadrian sarcophagus, where it has never belonged.

307   A nereid riding on a sea-horse, surrounded by cupids.

346   Bacchante performing an ecstatic dance and brandishing a thyrsus. Fragment.

353   Venus visiting Anchises. Relief in the British Museum.

*   *   *

On the wall opposite the window are displayed fragments of the relief frieze on *Trajan's Column,* raised in the Forum Trajanum (completed A. D. 113) to commemorate the emperor's conquest of Dacia. The fragments comprise heads of the god of the river Danube wearing a wreath of rushes (No. 323), of the emperor Trajan (No. 324), of Roman priests and soldiers (Nos. 325-28), of Dacians (Nos. 330-332,

335), and of Sarmatian horsemen (No. 333); see also No. 336, Room LXI, and No. 322, in the Storage Corridor. Also displayed are fourteen heads of Romans from the *Arch of Titus* and other monuments from imperial Rome (Nos. 308-21).

ROOM LXI

CASTS OF ANTIQUE SCULPTURE

98 Head of a panther.

RELIEFS

151 Fragment. Head of a man.

201 Fragment. Ideal head.

202 Fragment. Head of a man.

256 Nine heads from a procession of gods on a well-head (puteal). Museo Capitolino.

269 Fragment. Two men sacrificing.

282 Fragment showing two bacchic masks.

283 Fragment showing a head of Medusa.

284 Fragment. The face of Antinous. Villa Albani, Rome.

291 Three victorious Greek athletes. Above two of them are the names Demetrios and Menestheus. The Vatican.

296 Four heads from the so-called Medici vase. Florence.

300-301 The children of Niobe. From the lid of a sarcophagus in the Vatican.

305 Hercules Silvanus. Palazzo Rondanini, Rome.

336 Eighteen fragments of the Trajan Column, Rome, showing horses and cattle (cf. Room LX).

339 Head of a Roman of the Antonine period, formerly held to be that of the satirist Persius. Villa Albani, Rome.

340 Fragment. A griffin.

343 Fragment. Spring, personified as a woman.

344 Paris carrying off Helen in a quadriga.

347 Young satyr playing with a kid.

348 Fragment. Dancing woman.

349 Fragment. Bearded bacchic figure.

350 Fragment. A quadriga.

351 Fragment. Racing chariot passing a goal-post (meta).

352 The Tabula Iliaca. Representation of the Trojan War,
     probably used for teaching. Fragment found near the
     Via Appia. Now in the Museo Capitolino.

354 A Greek fighting with amazons.

605 Fragment. Bearded man.

606 Fragment. Hercules (?).

WORK BY THORVALDSEN

127 Sketch model for the statue of Elector Maximilian I
     of Bavaria. Original model.

BUSTS FROM THE TIME OF THORVALDSEN

J.J.Busch. The poetess Friederike Brun. Rome 1796. Cast.

Domenico Cardelli. Portrait of a lady. Original model (?).

— Countess Sophie Magdalene Knuth, née Moltke. 1796.
     Cast.

J.H.Dannecker. Schiller. 1794. Cast.

David d'Angers. Goethe. Colossal head. 1821. Cast.

C.D.Rauch. Goethe. 1820. Cast.

C.F.Tieck. Goethe. 1801. Cast.

Alexander Trippel. Dorothea Schlözer (?). Cast.

Unknown artist. Jean-Jacques Rousseau, in Armenian dress.
     Cast.

STORAGE CORRIDOR

In this corridor are stored those items of the collections of casts and sculptures of more recent date for which there is no room in the main collection, and which are here accessible for study. The corridor also contains a few original works by Thorvaldsen, mostly of minor interest, replicas, duplicate casts, etc. There can obviously be no fixed arrangement of the items stored here, but the following may be mentioned. Unless otherwise described, they are of plaster.

WORKS BY THORVALDSEN

83 STATUE. Christ. Half-size sketch model for the monumental statue (cf. No. 82, in the Christ Hall). Probably modelled by *Pietro Tenerani* in 1821, from Thorvaldsen's design and under his direction.

94 —The apostle Judas Thaddæus. First version of the statue, modelled by *Giuseppe Pacetti* in Thorvaldsen's studio in 1823, and altered in 1827. Later rejected by Thorvaldsen, and replaced by No. 105 in the Christ Hall.

95 —The apostle Andrew. First version of the statue, modelled by *Joseph Hermann* in Thorvaldsen's studio in 1823. Later rejected by Thorvaldsen, and replaced by No. 108 in the Christ Hall.

209 BUST. Portrait of a man. Colossal bust. Original model, c. 1804-05. Formerly described as a portrait of A. P. Bernstorff.

A869 —Elisa von der Recke. Half size. Probably executed during the winter of 1805-06. Marble (Thorvaldsen). Purchased 1931.

A703 —Auguste Böhmer. Marble (Thorvaldsen). Executed 1811-14 on the basis of C. F. Tieck's bust (cf. No.

28 A, p. 135); intended for the monument for which
Thorvaldsen made the reliefs No. 614 A, Room XIII.

A 887 BUST. Ghazi 'L-Din Haidar, Padishah of Oudh. 1824.
Marble (Thorvaldsen). Purchased 1949.

519 RELIEF. The genius of Light. Medallion. Original
model, Nysø 1841. Design for a medal to be awarded
to distinguished scientists and artists, struck during
the reign of Christian VIII.

673 —Medallion. Design for the reverse of Christian VIII's
coronation medal.

EGYPTIAN RELIEFS

Casts taken from Egyptian obelisks in Rome: Nos. 204-22,
from the obelisk on Monte Citorio. – Nos. 223-33, from
the obelisk in the Monte Pincio gardens. – Nos. 234-52,
from the obelisk in the Piazza della Trinità de' Monti.

ROMAN ANTIQUITIES

No. 44, hermaphrodite. Reclining statue. The figure is antique, found in the thermae of Diocletian in Rome; the
mattress was carved by *Bernini* after another ancient sculpture. The original was formerly in the Villa Borghese, but
is now in the Louvre. – No. 54, fragment of a group. –
No. 96, an eagle. – No. 101, Jupiter Serapis. Colossal head.
From the so-called Albani bust in Munich. – No. 103, Minerva. Colossal head. – No. 122, head of the Farnese Hercules. The statue is in the museum in Naples. – No. 125,
the head of Ajax, from the group in the Vatican representing Ajax with the body of Patroclus. – No. 126, Mars.
Bust in the Louvre. No. 163, Antinous. Colossal bust, found
in Hadrian's villa; now in the Vatican. – No. 164, Antinous.
Colossal bust, in the Louvre. – No. 166, Antinous. Head
and shoulders of a colossal statue found in Hadrian's villa

in 1738; now in the Museo Capitolino, Rome. – No. 173, the emperor Lucius Verus. – No. 186-87, Roman portraits. – No. 193, Julius Caesar. – No. 322, the goddess of Victory recording the deeds of the Romans on a shield, between two trophies of Dacian weapons. Reliefs from Trajan's Column (cf. Room LX).

FROM THE RENAISSANCE PERIOD

No. 1, head of Michelangelo, from the studio of *Daniele da Volterra*. Probably a cast of the bronze head on the marble bust in the Museo Capitolino, Rome. – No. 2, Madonna Taddei. Tondo relief by *Michelangelo* in the Royal Academy, London. – No. 4, imaginary head. Architectural ornament of the 16th century. – No. 5, Salome dancing before Herod. Marble relief by *Donatello* in the museum at Lille. – No. 8, bowl with hunting scenes in arabesques. The original is of metal, of the 16th century. – No. 9, 16th century helmet (a so-called borgognotta), showing the judgment of Paris on one side, and the abduction of Helen on the other. – Nos. 12-13, heads of children, by *François Duquesnoy*. – Nos. 14-15 mask and bust of sleeping child, by *François Duquesnoy* or his school. – No. 97, pacing bull. Statuette by *Giovanni da Bologna*. Probably after a replica from the studio of *Francesco Lusini*.

18TH AND 19TH CENTURIES

2 *Angelo Bezzi*. A little dice-player. Statue. Marble.
21 *Francis Chantrey*. Sir Walter Scott. Colossal bust. Cast.
21 A *J. H. Dannecker*. Schiller. Colossal mask. Cast.
    John Flaxman. Henry Philip Hope, brother of Thomas Hope. Bust. Marble. Purchased at the Hope auction in England, 1917.
3 *Pietro Galli*. The youthful Bacchus. Statue. Marble.

5 *Pietro Galli.* Olympus, the inventor of the flute. Statue. Marble.

23 A *Hermann Schievelbein* (?). Karl Freiherr von und zum Stein. Bust. Cast. Presented in 1870 by Herr Eichler, plasterer, Berlin.

Johan Tobias Sergel. The painter N. Abildgaard. 1794. Portrait medallion. Cast.

30 *Filippo Tagliolini* (?). Colossal female head. Modelled for the restoration of the antique so-called Farnese Flora, in the museum in Naples. Cast.

27 *Pietro Tenerani.* Pope Gregory XVI. Bust. Cast.

28 A *C. F. Tieck.* Auguste Böhmer. 1804. Bust. Cast. (Cf. Thorvaldsen's marble bust of the same subject, No. A 703, p. 133, executed on the basis of the present bust).

Alexander Trippel. The painter N. Abildgaard. Rome, c. 1776-77. Bust. Cast. The original is in the Academy of Fine Arts, which presented the present bust to the Museum in 1941.

26 *Emil Wolff.* Karl Josias von Bunsen. Bust. Cast.

Unknown artist. Thorvaldsen. Bust. Lent by the Ny Carlsberg Glyptotek, 1943. (Cf. the marble version in Room XXXVIII).

9 *Unknown artist.* K. F. Schinkel, the architect. Portrait medallion. Zinc.

Unknown (British?) artist. Silence. Statue. Marble. Purchased at a sale in London 1920.

Unknown (Polish?) artist. The death of Prince Jozef Poniatowski. Relief.

DANISH ARTISTS

H. V. Bissen. The poet Ludvig Bødtcher. 1826. Bust. Purchased 1926.

19 —Thorvaldsen. 1831. Bust. Cast.

32   *C.Christensen*. Thorvaldsen, standing leaning against his own statue of Hope. After Thorvaldsen's self-portrait statue. 1845. Medallion. Model for a medal to be struck on the occasion of Thorvaldsen's death.

33-34   The goddess of Victory in her quadriga. Two medallions, inscribed respectively "D.V.Januar" and "Juli 1845". Designs for the above mentioned medal. The finished medal is the work of *H.Conradsen* (see the specimens in bronze and silver in the showcase in Room XXXI).

G.C.Freund. Cupid and Psyche. Modelled in 1887 from a relief believed to have been made by Thorvaldsen in Dresden in 1841. Presented by G.C.Freund, 1887.

Andreas Paulsen. The archaeologist Georg Zoëga. Portrait medallion. Marble. Purchased 1887.

T.Stein. Thorvaldsen's valet, C.F.Wilckens. 1871. Bust. Marble. Presented by the artist, 1877.

Thorvaldsen. Portrait of a man. Bust. Marble. Copy made by *T.Stein* of No. 226B, Room XXXVII, formerly believed to represent Georg Zoëga. Purchased 1898.

TRIAL PANELS

The Storage Corridor also contains a number of panels with motifs from the decorations on the facades of the Museum.

One of the panels, showing two workmen carrying a relief and a bust, was cut out of Sonne's original wall frieze in 1907, and mounted in an iron frame.

The other panels were experiments for the restoration of the facades; most of them were placed out of doors in order to test the durability of the method used.

Five of the panels have the same motif from Sonne's

frieze: the painter N.F.Habbe and the sculptress Adelgunde Herbst looking at one of Thorvaldsen's reliefs, which a workman is carrying. These panels were made in 1899 and 1900, four of them of slabs of coloured terracotta. The slabs for two of the panels were made by *J.F.Willumsen* at Ville-roy & Boch's potteries at Merzig, near Trier, *Villeroy & Boch* themselves sent a panel, and the fourth panel was made at the P.Ipsens Enke pottery by *O.Mathiesen* (later factory manager at the Royal Copenhagen Porcelain Manufactory) for *J.F.Willumsen,* and under the latter's supervision. The fifth panel with this motif is composed of coloured plates of glass set in black cement mortar. This experiment was carried out by the glazier *H.A.G.Fledelius.*

The painter *Axel Johansen* carried out experiments with panels of coloured plaster (the same technique as was used for the original Sonne frieze, and for the recent recreation of it on the wall). The panels showing two workmen drag-ging a piece of sculpture, and two women with a child, are two of his experiments.

On the wall to the right of the door leading to Room XLIX is the trial panel by the painter *Oscar Willerup* of Son-ne's frieze executed in mosaic, showing a boy with a dog (1899).

The panel from the frieze of chariot-racing genii in the courtyard was executed experimentally in "Deckosit" in 1934 by the painter *Harald Hansen.*

*   *   *

INDEX OF WORKS BY THORVALDSEN

STATUES, MONUMENTS, AND SKETCH MODELS FOR THESE

Jason: No. 52 (p. 32). No. 51 (p. 43).

The preaching of John the Baptist: Nos. 59-70 (p. 32). Nos. 71 (p. 32). No. 72 (p. 32). Nos. 73-81 (sketch models) (p. 82).

Seated lady (sketch models): Nos. 168-69 (p. 86).

Seated lady with a boy (sketch model): No. 170 (p. 86).

Eugène de Beauharnais, Duke of Leuchtenberg: No. 156 (p. 30).

The genii of Life and Death (sketch model): No. 157 (p. 82).

The genii of Life and Death beside a meta (sketch model): No. 158 (p. 82).

The Lucerne lion: No. 119 (p. 33).

Recumbent lion: No. 122 (p.33). No. 121 (p. 49).

Luther (sketch model): No. 160 (p. 86).

Mars and Cupid: No. 7 (p. 32). No. 6 (p. 44).

Maximilian I: No. 128 (p. 30). No. 127 (sketch model) (p. 131). No. 129 (p. 33). Nos. 530-31 (p. 31).

Melanchton (sketch model): No. 161 (p. 86).

Mercury about to kill Argus: No. 5 (p. 32). No. 4 (p. 46). No. 5A (sketch model): (p.85).

Minerva (sketch models): Nos. 17-18 (p. 85).

Mother and two children: No. 651 (p. 104).

Triumphant Muse (sketch models): Nos. 49-50 (p. 82).

Nemesis (sketch model): No. 19A (p. 82). No. 19 (p. 85).

Countess Ostermann: No. 166 (p. 47). No. 167 (p. 60).

Achilles and Penthesilea: No. 657 (p. 103).

Pope Pius VII: Nos. 142-45 (p. 30). Nos. 146-47 (p. 33). Nos. 148-49 (sketch models) (p.85).

Jozef Poniatowski: No. 123 (p. 29). No. 125 (p. 33). No. 124 (p. 47). No. 126 (sketch model) (p. 76).

Wlodzimierz Potocki: No. 155 (p. 33). No. 155A (p. 51). No. 361 (p. 35). No. 627 (p. 38).

Cupid and Psyche reunited: No. 27 (p. 41). No. 28 (p. 59).

Psyche with the jar of beauty: No. 26 (p. 59). No. 25 (p. 77).

Little girl (Jeanina Stampe) represented as Psyche: No. 174 (p. 60).

Georgiana Elizabeth Russell: No. 173 (p. 60). No. 173A (p. 70).

Schiller: Nos. 135-37 (p. 30). No. 526 (p. 36). No. 138 (sketch model) (p. 85).

Monument to General Schwarzenberg (sketch model): No. 120 (p. 85).

Shepherd boy: No. 176A (p. 54). No. 177 (p. 60). No. 177A (sketch model) (p. 82).

Sibyl (sketch models): Nos. 57-58 (p. 82).

Little girl (Jeanina *Stampe*) represented as Psyche: No. 174 (p. 60).

Terpsichore: No. 653 (p. 104).

Thorvaldsen, self-portrait statue: No. 162 (p. 33). No. 162 A (p. 54). No. 163 (sketch model) (p. 86).

Venus with the apple: No. 11 (p. 42). No. 12 (p. 59).

Venus and Cupid (sketch model): No. 13 A (p. 82).

Venus and Cupid: No. 656 (p. 105).

Victory (sketch model): No. 48 (p. 85).

Vulcan: No. 9 (p. 32). No. 8 (p. 45). No. 10 (sketch model) (p. 85).

Youth with a dog (sketch model): No. 185 (p. 82).

COPY FROM THE ANTIQUE

Pollux: No. 655 (p. 106).

PORTRAITS

BUSTS

Alexander I: No. 246 (p. 48).

St *Apollinaris:* No. 186 (p. 33).

Christian, Duke of *Augustenborg:* No. 203 (p. 47).

Frederik, Prince of *Augustenborg:* No. 205 (p. 34).

Baden, Jacob: No. 221 A (p. 34).

Baillie, Alexander: No. 262 (p. 61).

Barjatinsky, Maria Fjodorovna: No. 250 (p. 61).

Barlow, George Hilaro: No. 289 (p. 48).

Bartholin, Caspar: No. 227 (p. 60).

Bentinck, William: No. 261 (p. 67).

Bernstorff, A. P., 1795: No. 661 (p. 103).

The same, 1797: No. 662 (p. 103).

The same, 1804: No. 207 (p. 48).

The same (?), colossal bust: No. 209 (p. 132).

Böhmer, Auguste: No. A 703 (p. 132).

Bonar, Thomson Henry: No. A 893 (p. 47).

Bourke, Edmund: No. A 900 (p. 35).

Brandt, Henri François: No. 241 (p. 48).

Bray, François Gabriel de: No. 300 (p. 61).

Brun, Ida: No. 218 A (p. 52). No. 218 (p. 60).

Butera, Prince of: No. 275 (p. 34).

Butera, Princess of: No. 276 (p. 34).

Byron: No. 256 (p. 34). No. 257 (p. 48).

Caldoni, Vittoria: No. 279 (p. 53).

Camuccini, Vincenzo: No. 281 (p. 55). No. 282 (p. 76).

Queen *Caroline Amalie* (as princess): No. 198 (p. 54).

Princess *Caroline:* No. 193 A (p. 53). No. 193 (p. 56).

MEDALLIONS

DRAWINGS

COPIES FROM THE ANTIQUE

RELIEFS, AND SKETCH MODELS FOR THESE

Brisëis led away from *Achilles*,
1803: No. 489 (p. 43). No. 490
(p. 64).

Brisëis led away from *Achilles*,
1837: No. 491 (p. 35).

The centaur Chiron teaching
Achilles to throw a spear:
No. 488A (p. 52). No. 488
(p. 57).

Achilles binds the wounds of
Patroclus: No. 493 (p. 43).
No. 494 (p. 64).

Achilles with the dying amazon
Penthesilea: No. 495 (p. 43).
No. 496 (p. 64).

Achilles and Priam: No. 676
(p. 104).

Priam pleads with *Achilles* for
Hector's body: No. 492A
(p. 43). No. 492 (p. 64).

The sea-goddess Thetis dipping
her son *Achilles* in the Styx:
No. 487 (p. 35).

Actæon: No. 461 (p. 64).

As above: No. 461A (p. 64).

Diana and *Actæon*: No. 460
(p. 63).

Adam and Eve with Cain and
Abel: No. 551 (p. 36).
No. 552 (sketch model)
(p. 83).

Adonis: No. 476 (p. 64).

Hygiea feeding the snake of
Æsculapius: No. 318 (p. 31).
No. 322 (p. 44).

The *Ages* of Man and the Seasons: Nos. 638–41 (p. 54).
Nos. 642–45 (p. 66).

The *Ages* of Love: No. 426
(p. 41). No. 427 (p. 83).

Alexander the Great's triumphal
entry into Babylon: No. 503
(p. 31). Nos. 504, 505 (p. 35).
Nos. 506–7 (p. 36). Nos. 508,
509 (p. 64). Nos. 510–11, 512,
513 (all p. 65). No. 503 A
(p. 124).

Alexander induced by Thaïs to
set fire to Persepolis, 1832:
No. 514 (p. 51). No. 515
(p. 65).

As above, 1837: No. 516 (p. 36).

Cupid received by *Anacreon*.
Winter: No. 414 (p. 42).
No. 415 (p. 63).

Adaption of the above: No. 416
(p. 46).

Hector's farewell to *Androma-
mache*: No. 501A (p. 44).
No. 501 (p. 64).

Perseus on Pegasus rescuing
Andromeda: No. 486 (p. 44).

Hovering *angels* with flowers
and garlands: Nos. 590–91
(p. 66).

Three hovering *angels* (See:
Font): No. 555 (p. 74).

Angels playing: No. 587 (p. 41).
No. 588 (p. 65).

Angels singing: No. 585 (p. 41).
No. 586 (p. 65).

The *Annunciation*: No. 569
(p. 39).

Apollo: No. 326 (p. 46).

Apollo and Daphne: No. 478
(p. 64).

Apollo among the shepherds: No. 344 (p. 83).

Art and the light-bringing genius: No. 517 (p. 40).

Art and the light-bringing genius. A genio lumen. No. 518 A (p. 55). No. 518 (p. 65).

The protection of the *Arts* and Sciences: No. 607 (p. 83).

Genii strewing flowers on the symbols of the *Arts* and Sciences: No. 610 (p. 84).

Atalanta: No. 473 (p. 64).

Cupid and the youthful Bacchus treading grapes. *Autumn:* No. 412 (p. 42). No. 413 (p. 63).

Manhood, *autumn:* No. 640 (p. 54). No. 644 (p. 66).

Bacchante with a bird: No. 648 (p. 84).

Bacchante and a child satyr: No. 354 (p. 46). No. 355 (p. 62).

Satyr dancing with a *bacchante:* No. 357 (p. 50).

Similar subject: No. 358 (p. 50).

Cupid and *Bacchus:* No. 409 A (p. 42).

Adaptation of the above: No. 407 (p. 46). No. 408 (p. 63).

Cupid and the youthful *Bacchus* treading grapes. Autumn: No. 412 (p. 42). No. 413 (p. 63).

Mercury brings the infant *Bacchus* to Ino: No. 347 A (p. 50). No. 346 (p. 69). No. 347 (p. 62).

Brisëis led away from Achilles, 1803: No. 489 (p. 43). No. 490 (p. 64).

Brisëis led away from Achilles, 1837: No. 491 (p. 35).

Callisto: No. 472 (p. 64).

The *child's* guardian angel (For the school collecting-box in the Church of Our Lady): No. 596 (p. 40).

Childhood, spring: No. 638 (p. 54). No. 642 (p. 66).

Children praying: No. 628 (p. 66).

Marble *chimney-piece* with two caryatids and a frieze of cupids: No. 649 (p. 84).

Chione and Dædalion: No. 464 (p. 64).

The centaur *Chiron* teaching Achilles to throw a spear: No. 488 A (p. 52). No. 488 (p. 57).

The baptism of *Christ* (See: Font): No. 555 (p. 74).

As above, 1820: No. 557 (p. 56).

As above, 1842: No. 573 (p. 40).

Christ blessing the children (See: Font): No. 555 (p. 74).

Christ blessing the children: No. 566 (p. 83).

Christ and the two disciples at Emmaus, 1818: No. 562 (p. 65).

Christ with the two disciples at Emmaus, 1839: No. 563 (p. 56).

Christ's entry into Jerusalem, 1839-40: No. 559 (p. 39).

may be the queen of flowers:
No. 393 (p. 42). No. 394
(p. 63).

Cupid writes the laws of Jupiter:
No. 391 (p. 50). No. 392
(p. 63).

Cupid with the tamed lion:
Nos. 387, 387A (p. 63).

Cupid the lion-tamer: No. 388
(p. 42).

Cupid on earth, as the lion-
tamer: No. 378 (p. 52).
Nos. 382 (p. 62).

Cupid riding on a lion: No. 389
(p. 50). No. 390 (p. 63).

Cupid making a net to catch a
butterfly: No. 397 (p. 42).
No. 399 (p. 57).

Cupid and Psyche: No. 450
(p. 57).

Cupid and Psyche (relief series
for Palazzo Torlonia): Nos.
433-48 (p. 63).

Cupid and Psyche, "Goodbye to
Nysø": No. 449 (p. 84).

Psyche with the lamp approaches
the sleeping *Cupid*:
No. 429 (p. 41).

Cupid leaves the bed of the
sleeping Psyche: No. 428
(p. 41).

Cupid revives the swooning
Psyche: No. 430 (p. 41).
No. 431 (p. 63).

Cupid holding out a rose, and
concealing thistles: No. 405
(p. 67).

Adaptation of the above:
No. 406 (p. 54).

Cupid sailing: No. 400 (p. 63).

Adaptation of the above:
No. 401 (p. 70).

Cupid collecting shells for a
necklace: No. 402 (p. 45).

Cupid sets stone on fire: No. 404
(p. 63).

Cupid charms flowers from
stony ground: No. 403 (p. 45).

Cupid with a swan, and boys
picking fruit. Summer:
No. 410 (p. 42). No. 411
(p. 63).

Cupid riding on a swan: No. 421
(p. 54).

Cupid on a swan: No. 422 (p. 48).

Cupid's swan-song: No. 456
(p. 57).

Cupid stung by a bee complains
to Venus: No. 417 (p. 50).
No. 417A (p. 63).

Adaptation of the above:
No. 418 (p. 46).

Cupid's arrows forged in Vulcan's smithy: No. 419 (p. 46).
(Cf. No. 420).

Venus, Mars, and *Cupid* in Vulcan's smithy: No. 420 (p. 35).

Three *cupids* with a garland:
No. 592 (p. 66). No. 649
(p. 84).

Apollo and *Daphne:* No. 478
(p. 64).

Chione and *Dædalion:* No. 464
(p. 64).

Day: Aurora with the genius of
Light: No. 368 (p. 45).
No. 370 (p. 62).

The centaur Nessus embracing
the struggling *Deianira:* No.
480 (p. 52). No. 481 (p. 57).

518 A (p. 55). No. 518 (p. 65).

The genius of *Light*, design for a medal: No. 519 (p. 133).

The genius of *Light* with Pegasus: No. 327 (p. 40).

Medicine: No. 541 (p. 65).

Music: No. 535 (p. 65).

Navigation: No. 539 (p. 65).

The *New Year:* No. 548 (p. 40).

Painting: No. 520 (p. 58).

The genius of *Peace* and Liberty: No. 529 (p. 36).

Poetry: No. 532 (p. 65).

Poetry, 1844: No. 527 (p. 58).

Poetry (for the Byron monument): No. 131 (p. 50). No. 134 (p. 62).

Poetry (for the Schiller monument): No. 136 (p. 30). No. 526 (p. 36).

Poetry and Harmony: No. 528 (p. 55).

Three genii. *Regna firmat pietas,* the motto of Christian IV: No. 153 (p. 83).

Religion: No. 545 (p. 65).

Sculpture: No. 522 (p. 58). Similar subject: No. 523 (p. 58).

The genius of *Sculpture* seated on the shoulder of the statue of Jupiter, chalk sketch on a slate: No. 524 (p. 79).

Trade: No. 540 (p. 65).

Tragedy: No. 533 (p. 65).

War: No. 538 (p. 65).

"*Goodbye* to Nysø": No. 449 (p. 84).

The *Graces* dancing: No. 374 (p. 46).

The hovering *Graces:* No. 338 (p. 72).

The *Graces* listening to Cupid's song: No. 601 (p. 55). No. 602 (p. 66).

The *Graces* with Cupid in chains of roses: No. 375 (p. 42). No. 376 (p. 62).

Mnemosyne with *Harpocrates:* No. 337 (p. 53).

Love and *Health:* No. 373 (p.68).

Hebe gives Ganymede the cup and pitcher: No. 351 (p. 50).

Hercules receiving the draught of immortality from *Hebe:* No. 317 (p. 31). No. 321 (p. 44).

Hector's farewell to Andromache: No. 501 A (p. 44). No. 501 (p. 64).

Hector with Paris and *Helen,* 1809: No. 499 A (p. 44). No. 499 (p. 64).

Hector in *Helen's* chamber reproaches Paris for his cowardice 1837: No. 500 (p. 35).

Heliodorus driven out of the temple: No. 675 (p. 104).

Hercules receiving the draught of immortality from Hebe: No. 317 (p. 31). No. 321 (p. 44).

Hercules and Omphale: No. 677 (p. 105).

Hero with a slain lion: No. 475 (p. 64).

Homer singing for the people: No. 502 (p. 44).

The genius of *Light* with Pegasus: No. 327 (p. 40).

The Ages of *Love:* No. 426 (p. 41). No. 427 (p. 83).

Love and Health: No. 373 (p.68).

St *Luke:* No. 577 (p. 36). No. 581 (p. 65).

St *Luke* with his symbol the ox: No. 583 (p. 36).

St *Luke* as the first Christian painter: No. 584 (p. 36).

The priest Hans *Madsen* and Johan Rantzau: No. 603 (p. 36).

Manhood, autumn: No. 640 (p. 54). No. 644 (p. 66).

St *Marc:* No. 576 (p. 36). No. 580 (p. 65).

Venus, *Mars,* and Cupid in Vulcan's smithy, 1814: No. 420 (p. 35).

As above, 1810: No. 419 (p. 46).

St *Matthew:* No. 575 (p. 36). No. 579 (p. 65).

Design for a *medal* to be awarded to distinguished scientists and artists, struck during the reign of Christian VIII: No. 519 (p. 133).

Design for the reverse of Christian VIII's coronation *medal:* No. 673 (p. 133).

Meleager: No. 474 (p. 64).

Mercury brings the infant Bacchus to Ino: No. 347A (p. 50). No. 346 (p.69). No. 347 (p.62).

Psyche taken up to heaven by *Mercury:* No. 432 (p. 77).

Minerva: No. 325 (p. 46).

Minerva protects Virtue and reveals Vice: No. 600 (p. 31).

Jupiter enthroned between *Minerva* and Nemesis: No. 316 (p. 48).

Minerva grants a soul to mankind created by Prometheus: No. 319 (p. 31). No. 323 (p. 44).

Mnemosyne with Harpocrates: No. 337 (p. 53).

Muses:

Calliope: No. 336 (p. 53).

Clio: No. 328 (p. 53).

Erato: No. 333 (p. 53).

Euterpe: No. 329 (p. 53).

Melpomene: No. 331 (p. 53).

Polyhymnia: No. 334 (p. 53).

Terpsichore: No. 332 (p. 53).

Thalia: No. 330 (p. 53).

Tragedy and Comedy: No. 342 (p. 55).

Urania: No. 335 (p. 53).

The dance of the Muses on Helicon, 1804: No. 341A (p. 124).

As above, 1816: No. 340 (p.41). No. 341 (p. 62).

Narcissus: No. 477 (p. 64).

Nemesis recites the deeds of men to Jupiter: No. 320 (p. 31). No. 324 (p. 44).

Jupiter enthroned between Minerva and *Nemesis:* No. 316 (p. 48).

Nemesis in a chariot, attended by the genii of Punishment and Reward: No. 364 (p. 51).

The centaur *Nessus* embracing the struggling Deianira: No. 480 (p. 52). No. 481 (p. 57).

Cupid revives the swooning *Psyche:* No. 430 (p. 41). No. 431 (p. 63).

Psyche taken up to heaven by Mercury: No. 432 (p. 77).

The priest Hans Madsen and Johan *Rantzau:* No. 603 (p. 36).

Rebecca and Eliezer at the well: No. 553 (p. 47).

Three genii. *Regna firmat pietas,* the motto of Christian IV: No. 153 (p. 83).

The *Resurrection* of Christ: No. 561 (p. 83).

The institution of the *Sacrament:* No. 558 (p. 56).

Satyr dancing with a bacchante: No. 357 (p. 50).

Similar subject: No. 358 (p. 50).

The protection of the Arts and *Sciences:* No. 607 (p. 83).

Genii strewing flowers on the symbols of the Arts and *Sciences:* No. 610 (p. 84).

Schiller's apotheosis: No. 135 (p. 30). (See: The Schiller-monument).

Baron *Schubart* bids farewell to his wife on her deathbed: No. 618 (p. 37). No. 618A (p. 47).

The *Seasons:* No. 683 (p. 104).

The Adoration of the *shepherds:* No. 570 (p. 39).

Shepherdess with a nest of cupids: No. 424 (p. 50). No. 425 (p. 80).

The Virgin's flight from the *Slaughter* of the Innocents: No. 571 (p. 65).

The judgment of *Solomon:* No. 554 (p. 83).

Childhood, *spring:* No. 638 (p. 54). No. 642 (p. 66).

Thorvaldsen with the *Stampe* family: No. 636 (p. 66).

Baron *Stampe* and his sons, Henrik and Holger: No. 637 (p. 66).

Cupid with a swan, and boys picking fruit. *Summer:* No. 410 (p. 42). No. 411 (p. 63).

Youth, *summer:* No. 639 (p. 54). No. 643 (p. 66).

Alexander induced by *Thaïs* to set fire to Persepolis, 1832: No. 514 (p. 51). No. 515 (p. 65).

As above, 1837: No. 516 (p. 36).

The sea-goddess *Thetis* dipping her son Achilles in the Styx: No. 487 (p. 35).

Thorvaldsen with the Stampe family: No. 636 (p. 66).

Tobias heals his blind father: No. 613 (p. 37).

Tombreliefs:

Andrea *Appiani:* No. 601 (p. 55). No. 602 (p. 66).

Vacca *Berlinghieri:* No. 613 (p. 37).

Philip *Bethmann*-Hollweg: No. 615 (p. 48).

Auguste *Böhmer:* No. 614 (p. 48). No. 614A (p. 50).

Countess *Borkowska:* No. 621 (p. 37).

Baroness *Chaudoir:* No. 624 (p. 38).

Cardinal *Consalvi:* No. 612 (p. 37).

Doomsday angels: Nos. 593-95 (p. 36).

Charles Drake *Garrard:* No.620 (p. 37).

Lady *Lawley:* No. 623 (p. 37).

Julius *Mylius:* No. 364 (p. 51).

The Earl of *Newburgh:* No. 622 (p. 37).

Princess *Poninska's* children: No. 616 (p. 37). No. 617 (sketch model) (p. 84).

Arthur *Potocki:* No. 628 (p.66).

Wlodzimierz *Potocki:* No. 627 (p. 38). No. 626 (p. 66).

Raphael: No. 611 (p. 36).

Baroness *Schubart:* No. 618 (p. 37). No. 618A (p. 47).

Anna Maria Porro *Serbelloni:* No. 619 (p. 49).

A *woman* ascends to heaven, above the genius of Death (Cf. Chaudoir): No. 625 (p. 38).

The Muses of *Tragedy* and Comedy: No. 342 (p. 55).

Ulysses receives the arms of Achilles: No. 497 (p. 46). No. 498 (p. 64).

Venus rising from the foam: No. 348 (p. 42).

Cupid stung by a bee complains to *Venus:* No. 417 (p. 50). No. 417A (p. 63).

Adaptation of the above: No. 418 (p. 46).

Venus, Mars, and Cupid in Vulcan's smithy, 1814: No. 420 (p. 35).

As above, 1810: No. 419 (p. 46).

Victory (hovering): No. 137 (p. 30). (See: The Schiller-monument).

Victory (sitting): No. 359 (p. 51). No. 360 (p. 62).

Variant of the above: No. 361 (p. 35).

Victory (standing): No. 362 (p. 51).

Variant of the above: No. 363 (p. 35).

The abolition of *villeinage:* No. 608 (p. 84).

Adaption of the above: No. 604 (p. 83).

Cupid received by Anacreon. *Winter:* No. 414 (p. 42). No. 415 (p. 63).

Adaption of the above: No. 416 (p. 46).

Old age, *winter:* No. 641 (p. 54). No. 645 (p. 66).

The *Virgin* and Child with John the Baptist (See: Font): No. 555 (p. 74).

The *Virgin* and Child with John the Baptist: No. 556 (p. 65).

The *Virgin's* flight from the Slaughter of the Innocents: No. 571 (p. 65).

Cupid's arrows forged in *Vulcan's* smithy: No. 419 (p. 46). (Cf. No. 420).

Venus, Mars, and Cupid in *Vulcan's* smithy: No. 420 (p. 35).

Youth, summer: No. 639 (p. 54). No. 643 (p. 66).

INDEX OF PORTRAITS BY OTHER ARTISTS
DEATH MASKS, AND LIFE MASKS

*   *   *

INDEX OF ARTISTS

whose work is to be found in the Museum.
(the numbers refer to pages).

INDEX OF ARTISTS 161

Michelangelo, 134.
Mila, Paul, 125.
Mohr, J., 118.
Monaco, Lorenzo, 95.
Müller, Adam, 75.
Møller, J. P., 72, 76.

Naldini, Pietro Paolo, 106.
Naucydes, 109.
Neergaard, Hermania, 75.
Nerly, F., 74, 118.
Neubourg, A.-C.-T., 125.
Noack, Wilhelm, 122.

Oehme, E. F., 70.
Oltos, 102.
Onofri, C., 120.
Oppenheim, M., 70.
Orsi, Lelio, 120.
Ottesen, O. D., 73, 79.
Overbeck, J. F., 70, 118.

Pacetti, Giuseppe, 132.
Pacetti, M., 68, 118.
Paggi, G. B., 120.
Paulsen, Andreas, 136.
Penthesilea painter, 102.
Perugino, 121.
Petzholdt, F., 72.
Pinturicchio, 95.
Piombo, Sebastiano del, 121.
Plagemann, C. G., 67.
Polyeuctus, 97.
Polygnotos, 102.
Polycleitus, 97, 109.
Praxiteles, 110, 114.
Prossalenti, Paolo, 128.

Raphael, 121.
Rauch, C. D., 126, 131.

Rauner, P. F., 127.
Rebell, J., 75.
Reinhardt, J. C., 69, 70, 118, 122.
Reinhold, H., 70, 118.
Rennie, George, 124.
Richardt, F., 75, 79.
Richter, J., 78.
Ricco, P., 126.
Riedel, A., 74, 77.
Riepenhausen, J., 118, 119.
Robert, Leopold, 68, 122.
Rubbi, J. J., 71.
Rørbye, M., 75, 79.

Sassoferrato, 95.
Savarelli, 128.
Scarsella, Ippolito, see Scarsellino.
Scarsellino, 120.
Schadow, F. W., 70.
Schick, G., 69, 118.
Schievelbein, Hermann, 135.
Schilbach, J. H., 70, 118, 122.
Schleisner, C., 117.
Scholl, Johann, 118, 119.
Scopas, 111.
Seidler, Louise, 80.
Senff, A., 71.
Sergel, J. T., 135.
Severn, Joseph, 76, 117.
Smith, L. A., 74.
Sonne, Jørgen, 74, 75, 121, 127.
Stanley, C. F. F., 123.
Stein, T., 136.
Steingrübel, J., 75, 122.
Stieler, J., 80.
Storelli, F., 119.
Suhrlandt, R., 78.
Sæbye, Poul, 58.

INDEX OF ARTISTS

who have participated in the decoration of the Museum building.
(the numbers refer to pages).

In addition, the painters *August Barlach* and *F. C. Lund* and the sculptor *Jacob Hallager* helped to execute the Sonne frieze on the exterior walls of the Museum, the painters *F. C. Lund* and *C. Købke* the ceiling decoration in Room XLI, and *William Klein* and *J. J. G. Guntzelnick* the ceiling decoration in Room XLII.

During the period 1936-40 the decorations in the courtyard of the Museum were renovated by the painter *Axel Johansen*, and after his death by the painter *Axel Salto*, assisted by *Hans Petersen*, foreman builder, under the direction of the architect *Kaare Klint*.

In April 1951 a complete restoration of the exterior walls was begun under the leadership of the City Architect, *F. C. Lund*, assisted by the architect *Johan Pedersen;* the task was completed in October 1959. It included the renovation of the Sonne frieze by the painter *Axel Salto*, assisted by the painters *H. C. Høier, Ib Asbjørn Olesen,* and *Jens Urup Jensen.* The original frieze was peeled off the wall and transferred to canvas by the painter Professor *Elof Risebye*, assisted by the painters *Poul Larsson, V. Rendal-Jensen, Robert Risager,* and *Erik Bøttzauw.*

*   *   *

The vignettes are reproductions in line-engraving of drawings by Thorvaldsen.

On the title page: Psyche kneeling before an altar. Sepia. Presumably a sketch for a relief for the Palazzo Torlonia.

P. 3: Cupid on a dolphin. Sepia. Cf. relief No. 379, Room XVI.

P. 8.: Sibyl. Sepia. Sketch for a statue (not executed). Cf. the sketch model No. 57, Room XXXIII.

P. 20: Nereid and sea-monster. Sepia.

P. 38: Seated man. Sepia.

P. 138: Cupid and Psyche. Sepia. Sketch for the statue (No. 27, Room II).

P. 162: Seated youth. Sepia.

*   *   *

CONTENTS

Indexes.

* * *

No. 162A. Thorvaldsen leaning against his statue "Hope". (Room xx).

The Thorvaldsen Museum, built by M.G. Bindesbøll, 1839-48.

Sonne's frieze: the facade facing Christiansborg Palace. (Restored 1951-59).

The Vestibule, showing the statues of Copernicus (l.) and Poniatowski (r.).

The courtyard of the Museum, with Thorvaldsen's ivy-clad tomb.

The Christ Hall, showing models for the statues in the Church of Our Lady.

Room XXXII, containing furniture from Thorvaldsen's residence at the
Royal Academy of Fine Arts, Charlottenborg.

View of the Corridor, First Floor. Models for statues and busts.

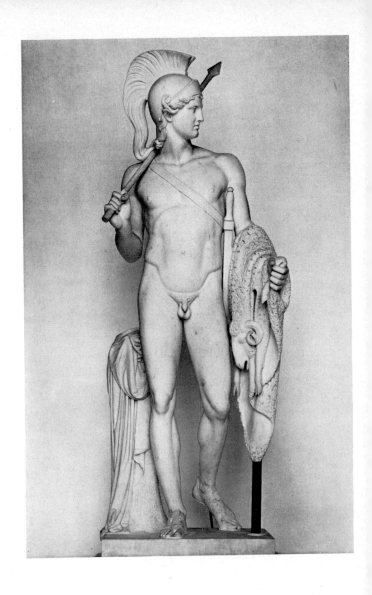

No. 51. Jason. Marble. (Room v).

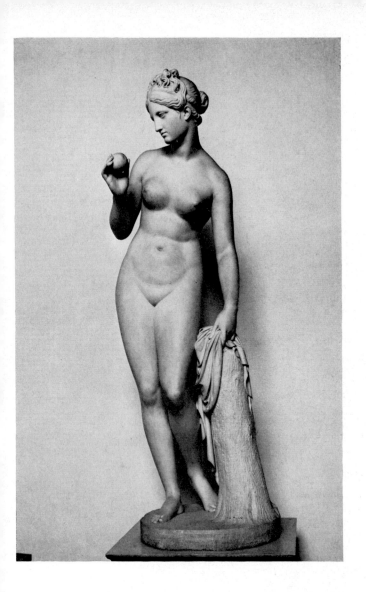

No. 11. Venus. Marble. (Room IV).

No. 27. Cupid and Psyche. Marble. (Room II).

No. 40. Ganymede. Marble. (Room 1).

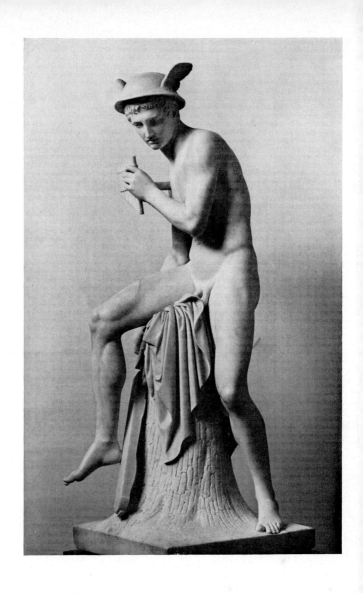

No. 4. Mercury. Marble. (Room x).

No. 176A. A shepherd boy. Marble. (Room xix).

No. 14. Hercules. Original model. (Stairs).

No. 149. Pope Pius VII. Sketch model. (Room LXII).

No. 44. Ganymede with Jupiter's eagle. Marble. (Room XIV).

No. 30. The Graces. Sketch model. (Room XXXIV).

No. 657. Achilles and Penthesilea. Sketch model. (Room LXII).

No. 369. Night. Original model. (Corridor, first floor).

No. 492A. Priam pleading with Achilles for the body of Hector. Marble. (Room v).

No. 370. Day. Original model. (Corridor, first floor).

No. 501A. Hector's farewell to Andromache. Marble. (Room VII).

No. 508. Section of the Alexander procession. Marble. (Corridor, first floor).

No. 414. Cupid received by Anacreon. Marble. (Room IV).

No. 508. Section of the Alexander procession. Marble. (Corridor, first floor).

No. 518A. Art and the light-bringing genius. Marble. (Room xx).

No. 450. Cupid and Psyche. Original model.
(Stairs).

No. 615. Monument of Bethmann-Hollweg. Original model. (Room XII).

No. 452. Cupid and Hymen. Original model.
(Stairs).

No. 553. Rebecca and Eliezer at the well. Original model. (Room XI).

No. 218A. Ida Brun. Marble. (Room XVII,.

No. 234. Prince Clemens Metternich. Marble. (Room XII).

No. 278A. Marchesa Florenzi. Marble. (Room XIII).

No. 257. Lord Byron. Original model. (Room XII).

No. 125. J. A. Koch: Apollo among the Thessalian Sherpherds. (Room XXIV).

No. 157. G. Schick: Heroic Landscape. (Room XXIV).

No. 113. P. Cornelius: The Entombment. (Room xxv).

No. 143. J. C. Reinhart: Italian landscape. (Room xxv).

No. 220. Const. Hansen: View of the temple of Poesidon at Pæstum.
(Room xxvi).

No. 238. Jens Juel: View of the Little Belt. (Room xxvii).

No. 209. C.W.Eckersberg: Alcyone's nurse.
(Room XXVI).

No. 253. J.T.Lundbye: Landscape at Arresø. (Room XXVI).

No. 242. J. A. Kraft: Carnival gaiety in a Roman street.
(Room XXVII).

No. 78. L. Fioroni: Evening scene at a Roman osteria. (Room XXIII).

No. 266. Ernst Meyer: A Roman street letter-writer.
(Room XXVIII).

No. 199. Blunck: Danish artists at the osteria La Gensola. (Room XXXI).

No. 227A. C. A. Jensen: Baroness Stampe.
(Room XXXII).

No. 184. J. C. Dahl: Norwegian mountain landscape. (Room XXII).